Lisa Bedbak lives in Ann Arbor, Michigan, with her husband, Ajjai, and sons, Arjun and Anmol.

This book is dedicated to my late maternal grandparents, Aja and Aie, for their unending love for me; to all the courageous women who found strength to write their beautiful memoirs and inspired me; to all the kids who don't stop dreaming; and to all the amazing people who carry innocence and compassion in their hearts and help others.

Lisa Bedbak

MY CRIES AND MY TRIUMPHS

AUSTIN MACAULEY PUBLISHERS™

LONDON • CAMBRIDGE • NEW YORK • SHARJAH

Ordering Information
Quantity sales: Special discounts are available on quantity purchases by corporations, associations, and others. For details, contact the publisher at the address below.

Publisher's Cataloging-in-Publication data
Bedbak, Lisa
My Cries and My Triumphs

ISBN 9781645753414 (Paperback)
ISBN 9781645753407 (Hardback)
ISBN 9781645753421 (ePub e-book)

Library of Congress Control Number: 2021900450

www.austinmacauley.com/us

First Published (2021)
Austin Macauley Publishers LLC
40 Wall Street, 33rd Floor, Suite 3302
New York, NY 10005
USA

mail-usa@austinmacauley.com
+1 (646) 5125767

My sincere thanks to my mother, my husband, my brother, and my two kids, Arjun and Anmol. Thank you for believing in me and always bringing out the best in me.

Introduction

This book carries the story of my childhood and a few glimpses of my early adulthood. I was told to be quiet and keep the skeletons in the closet. My uncertainties for the future and the vulnerabilities of the childhood were huge roadblocks in expressing the emotions building up in my aching heart. Writing my story has strengthened my own belief in humanity. Strangely, I felt nothing but pride when I wrote about my life. Who am I to judge? Who am I to even say that they are skeletons?

The heart-broken little girl buried inside me. Though the stories of our lives are all unique, our emotions connect us in this whole process of writing, I ended up helping that girl and our emotions resonate within each other despite our differences. I hope you connect with my life's story.

Chapter One

October 1988, Rampur, India

My mind was clouded with thousands of thoughts and my palms were wet with sweat on a warm Sunday evening in October. I had been working on a Biology project for almost over two weeks. The topic was based on food chain. I believed I had done an astounding job drawing some good pictures. I had to write the last paragraph and I wanted it in my best handwriting. I sat at the center of the floor in my tiny room and was surrounded by colored pencils, rulers, glue, and sticky notes. I hummed to myself as I sketched and wrote on my sheet. I was happy because it was almost dinner time. Mum was cooking lamb curry and rice. It was a tradition in our house those days to eat some lamb dish every Sunday. It was my favorite and my father's favorite, too.

As I tried to finish up my work on the three by three feet drawing sheet, I got even hungrier. The aroma from the kitchen had filled up our two-bedroom house. Mum and I had cleaned the whole house that morning. The cement floor reflected light. The cool breeze from outside waved the floral curtain on the front door a bit. The walls in our house were painted green and I could see my silhouette on the wall on my right side.

My father was watering the plants in small pots outside the window. Spending time in the garden was something my father never did. I was pleasantly surprised to see him do that. He didn't look angry either.

It was going to be a good day. Mum had almost finished cooking delish food. My father was helping Mum by taking care of the plants in the garden. My little brother, Joy, was playing with his toy train. He had just turned five and was a little bundle of energy. Everything looked perfect.

Two minutes later, I heard my father calling my name.

"Lisa, come here right now," he said in a loud voice.

As I looked outside the window, I could see the frown on his face. "Yes, Papa. Let me finish this sentence. I will be right there," I responded immediately.

"I want you to come here right now. There are two pieces of paper near the flower pots. How dare you throw these things here! Trash needs to be in the trash bag, not near the flower pots!" he screamed.

I knew it wasn't me. Maybe it was Joy, maybe those tiny pieces of paper flew in the air and got in the pot. But I was certain it was not me. I was about to put the pencil down and a plastic cover on my sheet when my father marched into my room.

I had started to shiver by then.

"I am coming, Papa. I will clean it up now," I said nervously.

Before I could finish my sentence, my father was tearing up my project work paper sheet into many pieces. He destroyed my hard work in five seconds. My good handwriting didn't look that good anymore in tiny pieces scattered all around the floor.

As I struggled to fight back my tears behind my innocent eyes, I got a tight slap on my face.

"This is what you get for not listening to your father. You are such a stubborn girl," he said.

His face was red. His eyes projected menace. His rage terrorized me. I never talked back when he was like that. I listened to whatever he said because I wanted to be done with it. The last thing I wanted was his rage to prolong. I didn't cry. The tears I was trying to fight back in my eyes evaporated.

I stood there like a statue, motionless and stolid, for a long time that evening. I was like a stone that never shone. I didn't feel the physical pain of the tight slap because I was numb from inside. A couple of hours later, we ate dinner in pin drop silence. It wasn't the picture of a perfect family. Far from it actually. It was as dysfunctional as it could be. The lamb curry and rice weren't tasty anymore. I kept looking at my dinner plate. I hated the sight of food, my life, and that house.

For almost an hour. I sat dissecting each grain of rice. I continued to look at my plate even after everyone was gone. I held myself culpable for not listening to him. I blamed myself and I felt miserable.

But no matter how hard I tried, I couldn't fathom why my father destroyed my project sheet. That sheet carried my sweat and labor. My two weeks of sheer hard work was ripped to shreds in just few seconds.

My father didn't drink alcohol, neither was he on drugs. He had always been like this as long as I could remember. His rages were sudden and inexplicable, yet my biggest challenge was not my father, it was to keep my unfaltering courage alive. I could feel the huge uphill battle within myself. My determination wandered aimlessly in a deep dungeon. The saddest part of all this was that my father never ever apologized. He always thought and assumed

11

that he was right. In fact, nobody talked to me about it. That's how things worked in my house. I was left alone to fend for myself. I was only eleven years old.

My father went to bed early that night after eating the sumptuous meal cooked by Mum. He started snoring in just ten-fifteen minutes.

The whole experience was so painful that when the pain traveled through my heart, it bled. But it also showed me the endless possibilities. Somethings in my life weren't right and I had to change them.

I learned that day that pain could be so ridiculously motivating. It was around eight thirty in the night when I sat down on the floor to start my project all over again. When Mum woke up to check on me, it was past midnight. She made me some coffee and sandwiches.

I was up until five in the morning next day. Once done with the project, I was too tired to even stand up. I hid that sheet of paper under my bed. I was running out of strength. I didn't have the strength to start it all over in case my father tore it again.

I really wanted to sleep for couple of hours before going to school but I changed my mind and went outside. The air was chilly. It was quiet, except for the chirping of the birds. The day was about to begin.

The sky looked pinkish red. Looking the sun rise from the horizon was just enough to stir up many powerful emotions in my young mind. As I watched the sun rise that morning, hope made me see things in a different light.

During my darkest days of childhood, when all doors closed on me, I could still cling to the unending thread of hope. I sincerely dreamt that someday I would be able to climb up that high wall of abuse and escape.

My Biology teacher was so impressed with my project that she ended up giving me 100 out of 100. She came to my desk and handed me the paper. I couldn't believe the score. I was happy, proud, and sad at the same time.

When we sat down for dinner that night, I told everyone my result. Nobody said anything about that. "You're not sitting properly for dinner," was all my father said in a sarcastic tone, because I kept dozing off.

Chapter Two

1977

My mum was only twenty-two when I was born on July 12th, 1977. The day was hot when I was born, Grandpa was working as an Accounts Officer in the Auditor General office.

As Mum and Grandma sat down in the back seat of the car, Mum looked worried.

"What's the matter?" Grandma asked.

"I don't know. There is something wrong with the baby's face. I can't see her eyes. All I see are two tiny lines."

"This baby weighs more than ten pounds. Look at her chubby cheeks. Most babies lose a pound or two in the first couple of weeks after they are born. Give her a few weeks. Once she loses a little weight, you will be able to see her eyes. Don't worry too much. You have a beautiful, healthy, sweet baby," Grandma assured Mum.

"Your baby is perfectly fine," Grandpa joined her, too.

So, that's how I came home to my grandparents' house from the hospital with my mum and maternal grandparents. My father was not there when I was born. He was two hundred and eleven miles away in Rampur, a small quiet town famous for coal mines.

In 1977, my father was working in Rampur as an accountant. My father worked for the Accounting Division in the Central Coalfields Office. There was only one hospital in Rampur those days and it was always crowded. Towards the end of Mum's due date, my father decided that Mum should move to her parents' house for few months.

Mum named me Lisa Leona Bedbak.

"Bedbak" is my father's surname. Lisa means "Elizabeth." Leona means "Lioness." Mum thought Lisa Leona Bedbak would go well together. But my nick name was "Lismun," a combination of Lisa and Moon!

My father came to see me after one month. Luckily, he was able to see me open my eyes and they didn't look like lines. Mum told me that he was happy to see that I was his spitting image.

Both Parents Away, 1980–1981

My earliest memory of my father was when I was around three and half years old. I was wearing a red frock and playing in the garden when I saw my father open the front gate of the house. I was so happy to see him that I started crying.

"Papa, I missed you so much. Why didn't you come for so long?" I asked him while he lifted me up in the air.

"I was busy with work," he said with a smile.

"But you are supposed to come and see me every month. Remember, you promised me last time."

"I will try to come more often now. Will that make you happy, Lisa?"

"Yes, Papa. Also, I don't like your beard. Can you please cut it?" I said while scrutinizing his face.

"You mean, shave my beard?"

"Yeah, that's the word I meant to say," I said with slight embarrassment.

I had a hard time saying words with "sh" when I was that young.

My father understood it well though. He smiled again as we walked into the house. It was my grandparents' house in Balangir, another small town in eastern India where my grandpa was posted in 1980-1981. It was a beautiful city with great cultural heritage. The house was a ranch style house and had a huge garden in the front. That was my favorite place to play.

Mum was married off when she was young. She was in the middle of her undergraduate program. It was an arranged marriage: a marriage, that is, fixed by the elders in the family or by friends. A distant relative of my grandpa got the marriage proposal for Mum. My father was a bright graduate student and was the Delhi University topper of his time. My mum's brother, Uncle Bhanja, knew my father well and vouched for his character and promising future. That's what they looked for in a groom in an arranged marriage those days. So, everyone thought he had great future prospects. When they got married, Mum was only nineteen and my father was twenty-three.

As Mum had not finished her degree before her marriage, she decided to finish it later and she did. But there were constant demands of money from my father's side of the family. The dowry system, where the bride's family gave money to the groom's family, wasn't unusual those days in India.

Once Mum completed her Bachelor degree, my father asked her to find a job as soon as possible. My maternal grandparents wanted to see Mum independent too, so they encouraged her to look for a job on her own.

Mum thought of becoming a teacher. But she had to finish her Bachelor in Education, B.Ed. program before that. There were no Bachelor of Arts programs in Rampur, so Mum had to stay away from my father in Balangir to finish her program. Even though my grandpa was posted in Balangir, Mum had to stay in a hostel dorm.

I was only three years old then. My grandparents offered to help my parents out. They said they would take care of me. My father loved the idea as he wasn't confident about taking care of a little girl. But he came and saw me every month. His visits were short for a couple of hours. I cried like hell when it was time for him to leave.

"This is not my house, Lisa. This is your mum's parents' house. I don't want to burden them. They are already doing a lot for you. I can't stay here longer," he explained it to me logically.

Once my father was gone, I got fever in the night because of separation anxiety.

Mum came and spent every weekend with me. When Mum was away, she became busy with her course work. That's when Grandpa stepped in and spent a great deal of time with me. His work schedule was for eight hours a day. Once his work was done, he spent all his free time with me. He read books to me and played hide and seek. But deep inside, I missed both my parents and wanted all three of us to live together.

I was a late talker and struggled to say even simple words. So, one of the doctors in Balangir told them that if they spoke to me a lot, I would be able to talk quicker. They talked to me all time. I had wrapped Grandma around my pinky finger.

One afternoon, I was taking a nap on a small, twin bed and my grandmother was sitting on the floor stitching buttons on a dress. I fell down but woke up immediately. I sat down immediately as if nothing had happened.

Grandma took me on her lap and asked in a very concerned voice, "Are you alright? You just fell on the hard, cement floor," she said.

Only then I began crying. I sat on her lap for that entire evening and didn't let her cook dinner. When Grandpa came home, there was nothing to eat, so he got food from outside and we enjoyed hot chicken kabobs. They protected me, dealt with my tantrums, and loved me unconditionally.

My First Asthma Attack

In December 1981, my grandparents decided to go to Bombay for a vacation. They asked Mum to join them. Mum had some project to do so she stayed back. But I tagged along with them. Me, Grandpa, and Grandma were happy when we boarded the train after dinner.

There was a slight chill in the air. Everything was okay until we went inside. Grandma had a special blanket for me that Mum had knitted. Grandpa found our little cabin and we were just settling down. Out of nowhere, I started projectile vomiting.

"Are you okay, sweet pie?" Grandma asked, holding me tight as if that would stop the vomiting.

"Looks like some sort of indigestion," Grandpa said, frowning with concern.

"My God, her skin is burning. Looks like she has high fever," Grandma said with more concern in her voice.

I was shivering and my fingertips were cold. The next thing my grandparents knew was that I struggling to breathe. My grandpa looked outside and fortunately, the train hadn't started.

We got off the train as soon as we could. I was admitted in the hospital that night. That was my first asthma attack.

Everything changed after that night. My asthma was triggered by cold air and pollution. Winters were bad for me as I got sick often. Mum was pretty deft in making woolen sweaters, gloves, and hats, so she made sure that I was covered in thick woolen clothes from head to toe when we went out.

Suffering from asthma also meant that I wasn't allowed to eat a lot of food that included dairy foods like ice-cream and yogurt. There were restrictions on eating banana and guava. I wasn't allowed to drink cold water and cold juice. So, Mum named those as "cough foods."

Mum had a really hard time accepting that I had asthma. Onetime, when we were in the doctor's office, Mum asked the doctor teary eyed, "She is so tired and sick these days. I am just so worried. Please tell me if my child will be able to lead a normal life."

I sat by her side, breathing from the mouth.

The doctor was nice and assured Mum, "Yes, ma'am. I think she will be fine. A lot of people outgrow their asthma when they become adults."

Mum had trained me well. I could say, "No," to cough foods even if my mouth was watering. I was little more than four, yet I had become an expert in talking about health.

When I had trouble breathing, it became impossible for me to sleep lying down. The only way I could sleep was sitting up. There were many sleepless nights like that. Not just for me but for Mum, too. For nearly that entire winter, for the whole three months, Mum slept in a sitting position. She put a lot of pillows behind her back and I slept on her, sitting. Then she got up in the morning and went to work. Every working day for those three months.

One night, Mum was totally exhausted, she looked at me, kissed my forehead.

"I think I will leave this program, so I can focus on you," she said.

But she didn't. Somehow, she managed to do both. Her training and focusing on me.

I noticed that Mum had become quiet. She seldom opened her books to read and she looked severely sleep deprived. There were days when she said, "Can you please sleep with grandmother tonight?"

But she knew I didn't like it much, so, most nights, it was just the two of us.

She had neither the energy nor the time to concentrate in her course. She was mostly drained taking care of a cranky, sick child. She had started to look stressed out, too. On top of that my father hardly visited us or called us. Mum had no idea where was her marriage going.

One night, when she came back from her training class, I said, "I want some hot soup."

Mum was tired, yet she said, "Okay, I will make it. No more demands after this. We are going to bed."

She took a long time in the kitchen but when she brought it, she poured the soup in the bathroom sink. She was half asleep and she had no idea what she was holding. She turned towards me and collapsed on the sofa. Clearly, she had too much stress in her life.

Mum's life was a vehicle, her fuel was her inner strength. I don't know how she could manage when the vehicle wasn't stable. I was worried about Mum but Grandma understood how tired her daughter was. That night, I slept with my grandparents. When I threw up in the middle of the night, they cleaned up everything.

The truth was that even though I was sick, I could see that my life was engulfed in love and utmost care. I was constantly surrounded by people who inspired me and pushed themselves harder to take care of me. I was living with people who made their way like a river through rocks.

Chapter Three

My First Friend

There weren't many English Medium schools in Balangir those days. I was admitted in a Catholic Convent School. Grandpa dropped me at school on his way to work and Grandma picked me up around three in the afternoon.

I liked the school. It was a yellow building surrounded by trees. There were pictures of Mahatma Gandhi and Jawaharlal Nehru in every classroom. I had a nice teacher and there were fewer kids. She was soft spoken and we called her "Teacher Rita."

I made a few good friends. There was a little girl, Tinky, who came from the other side of town. She was sweet, funny, and cute. I loved the little dimples on her cheek. We played silly games where I put my finger inside her dimples to see how far it went. We both shared infinite love for each other. In a way, we were both weird and loved to giggle endlessly, sometimes distracting other kids.

During recess, we made fun of each other and laughed at our silly jokes. Sometimes, we threw paper pieces at each other for no apparent reason. We played imaginary games and we counted each strand of hair on each other's head. Tinky taught me how to climb a tree and how to eat a mango without cutting it. It was my first friendship and the roots of love remained tight together.

One afternoon, Tinky had stopped by at our house after school to play with me. Her parents came in the evening to pick her up. She didn't know how to tie her shoe laces. Her father offered to tie them for her, but she insisted, "I want Mommy to tie my right shoe lace and Daddy to tie my left shoe lace."

Her parents bent down and happily tied her laces. I missed my father that night. I missed him a lot.

The next day when Mum came to spend the Christmas holidays with us, my first question was, "When am I going to see Papa next?"

"Very soon," Mum said.

I demanded more answers, so I asked again, "When are we going to stay together, all three of us?"

"Soon, my dear," Mum answered again patiently.

Mum stayed for ten days with us in December that year and I clung to her. I had missed her so much. I had learnt some rhymes, so I sang for her. I jumped and danced all the time because being with Mum was time for celebration for me. Mum was so happy that she asked me to sing the rhymes again and again.

I was glued to her the whole time. She liked it, too, I guess. We walked to the park every evening. I held her fingers tightly. And that feeling of security was the strongest wall around the castle, the castle I had built in my mind where I lived with Mum. I was one love starved child. I missed Mum immensely when she went back after the Christmas break.

Spring 1982, Rampur

Mum had her final exams in March but she decided to take me to Rampur for five or six days to spend some time with my father. I knew Mum did it for me. My father hadn't come to see me for many months and I missed him.

We didn't know that my father had invited his parents and his three younger siblings, too. I was expecting just the three of us to spend some time together as a family, so when I a saw the big crowd at his home, I asked him, "Papa, I thought it was just going to be the three of us."

He answered, "Well, you spend a lot of time with your mum's parents. It will be nice if you can spend some time with my parents, too. That's why they are here."

I didn't say anything but just looked at him. He continued, "Do you understand what I said?"

"Yes," I said.

"Yes, my dear. It is nice to know all members of the family," Mum smiled and said.

But the next day, Mum spent all her waking hours in the kitchen, cooking for everyone. I didn't like it. My father and mother hardly spoke to each other.

One day, Mum hadn't eaten her lunch and it was almost dinner time, she was busy doing several loads of laundry. I sat there and watched her. She turned towards me and smiled.

"How do you always smile? Aren't you tired?" I asked.

Mum took a break and sat down beside me on the steps.

"Yes, I am little tired. That's okay. But when you smile, you share your biggest gift. You share a part of you. Smile, my little one. Smile always," she said.

I smiled back. Nobody needed a smile more than her at that moment. I knew when I smiled back, it made her feel loved.

Even as a little girl, I could clearly see that nobody in Dad's family talked nicely to Mum. She was mostly confined in the kitchen, cooking for everyone.

My father's brother, who was in high school, said to me, "But the smoke in the kitchen is not good for you. You can play with us."

But I insisted on being with Mum. It made no difference to me when they treated Mum badly. I guess it is universal with all the kids. Kids like people who treat their mothers with respect.

Unfortunately, the smoke in the small kitchen made me cough. That incident made my father angry. He shouted at me, "Why are you so stubborn? Your Mum is cooking and that smoke is not good for you. Why don't you listen to anyone?"

I was crying hysterically and yet managed to say, "I am not going anywhere. I will stay with Maa."

A couple of days later, I heard some serious discussions about money. Mum was expected to bring in money from her parents. That's how the dowry system worked in India. But Mum stood her ground and refused to ask her father for more money.

"I am not going to ask my father for any more money. He has already helped us enough. That is not happening," she said assertively.

There was a big fight, and everyone shouted at her. The upshot of it was that Mum couldn't continue smiling. She cried and that made me cry, too. Mum ate alone. Mum and I slept in a separate bed.

Most days, during our visit, my father was okay with me, but he hardly spoke to Mum. That broke my heart little more. My mum was beautiful, sweet, young, and strong. When everyone saw imperfections in her, I saw nothing but perfections.

She woke up early every morning, cooked for us, cleaned our dishes, did the laundry, cleaned the house, fed all the family members, and took care of everything around her. She wore a smile on her face like a priceless diamond. Yet, she got rejection after rejection.

One evening, my father went shopping with his parents and bought a *saree* for his sister. When he came home, he showed it to Mum and asked, "What do you think about this *saree*? Do you think my sister will like it?"

Even before Mum could say something, my father's mother interrupted and said, "What is there to ask your wife? You bought the *saree* for your sister. Leave it at that. You have always been such a bright student, a great scholar, why do you ask other peoples' opinions?"

Mum went back to the kitchen with tears in her eyes. It was around that time my father asked Mum again to get some money from her parents.

"Ask your father to send some money," he said again. His voice sounded more serious.

Mum refused, "I am not asking my father for any money. Why should my father pay his son-in-law money? I am done with this dowry thing. He already paid for your living expenses when you were doing your masters in Delhi. I am not going to ask him for more money. Not today, not tomorrow."

"Well, you have to ask your father for the expenses I am paying here."

"What expenses?"

"The expenses when you live here."

Mum didn't believe it initially. But when he said for the second time, she understood that he was indeed serious about it. Eventually, when it sunk in after a day, she knew that there was no place for her in that house.

I didn't know how to deal with these grown-up arguments. To me, they sounded like weird games and crazy things. I had no idea about the seriousness of the problem. It was hard for me as a small kid. It was just mystifying for me when I was forced to deal with those situations and I hated it.

When Mum and I left his house, my father was having breakfast. I still had a ray of hope in my heart that my father was going to stop us from leaving. But he didn't. I kept looking at him with wistful eyes. Mum was holding me in one hand and a big suitcase on another.

As we walked out of the door, I continued looking at him until I couldn't see any longer. That was the first time I saw my father's impassive face. No emotion, nothing.

My Grandfather, Boats, and Roses

When we came back from Rampur, I often cried. I was overwhelmed with sad feelings and I didn't know how to express them in words.

The night before Mum went to her hostel, she tucked me in and said, "I know you feel upset about your trip to Rampur."

I began to sob and said, "I always thought Papa loved me, but he didn't even look at me when we left."

Mum said, "I think he was stressed out, and he didn't know what to say."

I didn't agree with her. "But you look at me whenever you are stressed out," I told her.

"We all make mistakes."

Mum and I hugged each other and fell asleep.

Next day, Mum left for her hostel. She was finishing up her last leg of the course, so I spent my time with my grandparents. I had turned into an irritable child and often threw tantrums.

One evening, I refused to eat dinner. I threw a big tantrum and didn't stop crying until late night. My grandparents felt helpless.

"Are you not feeling well, Lisa?" Grandma asked very lovingly. I didn't say anything and kept crying. They couldn't know what was bothering me, and I didn't know how to tell them why I felt so restless.

Finally, when I had drained all my energy, I asked Grandpa, "Why was Papa so mad? Do you think he was mad at me? Is it because I live far away from him? I love Papa and miss him. I want all three of us to live together. When will that happen?"

Grandma massaged my legs and gave me some warm milk to drink, that I refused. I just couldn't stop crying, the tears didn't stop flowing and I felt like nothing placated me.

Grandpa hugged me as if he felt my agony and said, "Sweetheart, I can see that it is your heart talking here. Your drooping eyes tell me that you are tired. I think you should go to sleep. But before that, let me tell you something, my dear. Sometimes, we have to make some hard decisions and choices in life. Your parents are young and are still settling down. Soon, all three of you will live together,"

He wiped my tears and wiped his, too. That night, we had our dinner on the front lawn under the star covered skies with the fireflies.

There was a small stream of water behind my grandparents' house in Balangir. I loved to watch the flow of water. Grandpa found time to walk with me most evenings. He loved water and said that it had a calming effect on his tired mind.

That weekend, we made small paper boats. I was thrilled because each boat was of a different color.

"I love all the boats, Grandpa," I said so happily. We sat near the water and watched our boats float there. The water looked serene, without many ripples.

"I love how the boats float, Lisa," he said

"Me, too. But I am kind of sad that the boats are drifting away. They are just going farther and farther. Are they ever going to come back to us?" I asked him, still looking at the cute paper boats we made.

"No, they are gone. But don't feel sad because they left you. Be proud that we made them so sturdy that they can float on their own," he said with a bright smile on his face.

My relationship with my grandparents was amazingly simple with a strong element of love in it. That love held the indomitable spirits of our lives together. I learnt so much just talking to them. Those days were some of the best days of my life.

The memories gave me hopes, courage, and dreams during my darkest times later in life. I thank God for those early childhood experiences every single day.

My grandparents had a garden in front of their house, and there were many rose plants. Grandma loved gardening. There were all types and colors of roses, small, big, white, yellow, pink, and some black roses, too. The beautiful colors fascinated me. I liked sitting on the steps of the front door and watching her water the plants.

The thing I loved most about Grandma was her calmness. She was breathtakingly beautiful; big eyes, flawless skin, and sweet smile. She carried an ocean full of self-confidence in her demure personality. Anyone who knew her well could vouch for it.

School was good, I was reading two grade levels up. My teacher said, "Lisa, my dear, you are a born leader. You will be the class monitor for the rest of the semester."

I took great pride in being in that position and did my job with due diligence.

Soon, it was spring time. There were flowers everywhere and plants blossomed. I was feeling better and everything looked perfect. Every Sunday afternoon, I set out to catch butterflies with my grandpa. But he insisted on letting them fly away, and I obliged. I loved those little creatures.

"We have no right to destroy them. Just look at them but then let them go gently," Grandpa and I agreed with him.

Mentally Preparing Ourselves

Mum thought if the three of us lived together as a family, my father would change. She knew I wanted it, too. Her infinite love towards me made her understand things that I didn't say. Like onetime, she found me drawing pictures where all three of us looked out of the window.

So, even though, deep inside, Mum knew that her marriage wasn't great, she held on to some hope that someday things would get better.

One night, Mum asked me, "Do you want to start kindergarten in Rampur?"

I said, "Yes, yes. That's exactly what I want."

Mum said, "Good. I am going to look for a job in Rampur."

But I also had my own doubts, so asked her, "Is Papa going to be mad when we live with him?"

"No, sweetie. Basically, he is a good man. Your father is very bright. He will be such a good influence on you. You have his genes. You will turn out to be very smart, too."

"But he was so mad at you last time. You were always in the kitchen."

"When you have guests in the house, that's what you do. You take care of them. And to answer your question, no, I will not be in the kitchen all the time. I will be back from school when you are back. We will spend all our evenings together. We are going to be happy. We all do mistakes. Your father did a mistake," Mum said with a big smile on her face.

I listened to her quietly.

As I spent my time dreaming how cool it was going to be to stay with both my parents together and start kindergarten, I also knew that I was going to be away from my grandparents, and that made me sad.

A couple months later, Mum went to Rampur for few days to take a job interview. I gave her a small drawing on a paper. I said, "Mum, this is a picture our house. Will you give it to Papa?"

Mum hugged me and said, "Yes, sweetie. I will."

Mum left after eating lunch with us. That evening, my grandmother made my favorite dinner; spicy potato curry and rice with green peas. As we were finishing up our meals, I looked at my grandpa and said, "I will miss you both when I leave this place. Will you come visit to me often?"

"We will miss you, too. But that's where you belong; with your parents," he said.

Fall 1982, Rampur, Odisha, India

Mum found a job in an elementary school in Rampur in fall 1982 and we moved there permanently. When we reached there, my father wasn't there to pick us up. It was getting dark and there weren't many people at the bus stop. We waited for a long time and finally managed to get a taxi. I cried all the way home because my father did not come to pick us up.

Things were okay for few days. Mum cooked whatever my father wanted to eat. She treated him like a king. She was tractable and did whatever he said. He told her what to buy for groceries, how much money to spend, and about the new neighbors.

"Why does he have to tell you what to do? I feel like he is bossing you around," I asked Mum.

"Nothing like that, sweetie. Your father and I are a team. We always have been, that's why, we tell each other what to do."

I didn't understand that part very well and soon forgot about it.

Watching movies in Rampur was a luxury because most days we didn't have electricity. I watched Coal Miner's Daughter when I was a little girl. The stark resemblances between her hometown and Rampur surprised me so much that I told my mother, "There is another Rampur in this world, and it is in the US."

I was surrounded with poverty and illiteracy. Layers of dark dust got deposited on the furniture every few hours if the windows were slightly open. But Rampur, being a coalmining town, had lots of jobs for people. There weren't many locals there. Most people had uprooted themselves from their respective states in India with hopes of finding employment. People who did manual work were called "loaders" as their job was to transport coal. They had wrinkles on their dried-up faces. There was almost no public transport in Rampur those days. Most families had two-wheeler scooters and motor bikes. A lot of officers in my father's office were given jeeps and cars. These vehicles were driven by the official drivers appointed by the coalmining office. If the officers did not use them, then the vehicles were used by their wives for shopping and for buying vegetables. My father was somewhere in the middle of the officers and loaders and he did not have a jeep.

One evening, I went walking with my parents to get the voting identity cards for them. It was almost two miles each way. I held my father's pinky finger all the way.

"What is this card, Papa?" I asked

"It is called voting identity card," He replied

"Why do we need it, Papa?"

"It's an identity card. We need these cards to buy groceries from a local store."

"Got it, Papa."

Those were good moments, just talking to my father like that, learning things from him. I had so much pain in my calf muscles that night and I found it impossible to fall asleep. Mum was stitching a sweater for me while watching T.V. I stood behind her and said, "My legs have become useless."

She took me on her lap, "Let me help you."

I was almost half asleep and was in no mood to talk. As Mum massaged my legs, it didn't take me long to drift into deep sleep.

A couple of weeks later, I was admitted in a convent school for kindergarten, some eight miles away from our house. The school bus I took went through all the big coalmines in Rampur. I didn't like the sight of black coals around me. It wasn't the coal that I found unbearable. The pollution level was high in Rampur and that made me sick. But I liked those long bus rides because I could drift away in my thoughts.

After the first day in school, I came back home and went straight to bed.

"Lismun, you need to eat your dinner before going to bed," Mum coaxed me.

"I am not hungry," I said with a melancholic face.

"Are you feeling okay?"

"I don't like Rampur. I don't like piles of black coals everywhere. I don't like the school."

"How were the teachers? And the kids?" Mum's face showed a worried frown.

"Teachers were good. Kids were okay I guess," I said, pretending to be sleepy.

"Lismun, you will be fine. It's a good school. Give yourself some time and you will make friends."

I was in no mood to listen to what Mum was saying. More than anything else, I missed my grandparents deep inside. Mum brought a plate of food to the bedroom and fed me.

Days passed and Mum remained busy balancing my health, her new job, home, cooking, cleaning, and everything else. Time flew by and I grew tall and thin like a weed.

I couldn't believe how my father had changed in just six months. He was quick to tell me that I hadn't done a good job if I didn't fold my blanket properly or if I spelled a word wrong. He expected me to remember the capitals of all the states, so when I remembered them all, he got mad because I didn't remember the country capitals. As a little girl, I found it ambiguous and didn't know what would make him happy.

The saddest part of this was a lot of it was directed towards Mum. I didn't like how my father was silent and cold towards me and Mum. When Mum talked to him about any topic, he pretended as if he didn't listen. Sometimes, he just said, "Let's not talk now."

He often found fault in what she did. He was quick to say, "This food tastes horrible!" or, "Is this how clothes are ironed? What a sloppy way of doing things!"

He never appreciated how hard Mum worked, not even once. But he never failed to humiliate or criticize her. Like he thrived on that. He derived some sort of pleasure when he put her down. With time, it dawned on me; we weren't a happy family. He wasn't affectionate towards me anymore, he stopped telling me stories and smiling at my silly jokes.

Most of the times, my father never told us why he wanted us to do any particular thing and why he didn't want something to be done. He was whimsical and we had to be extra careful around him.

One day, he declared, "We are going to be vegetarians. Nobody is going to eat meat in this family." So, Mum cooked only dishes with different varieties of vegetables.

A few days later, he changed his mind and said," What is this! This food is not edible!" and we became non-vegetarians again.

For some weird reason, he didn't like rainbows. But like any normal child, I was fascinated by rainbows and their colors.

The seven colors fascinated me. I could watch them for a long time. One day, my father found me watching one after slight rain. "What is that stupid thing you are looking at?" he derided me harshly.

"It's a rainbow, Papa. It's beautiful," I said while studying his face.

"Rainbows are nothing. I can't believe you are so stupid that you have to watch that silly thing."

I never watched rainbows again because it reminded me of my father's angry face.

He got mad when I became sick or had asthma attacks. We walked on eggshells all the time, never knowing what was going to trigger his anger. He got mad if the house was dirty, if the clothes weren't folded properly, if I watched T.V., and if I asked a lot of questions. Every once in a while, I made drawings and pictures but he didn't pay heed to the small creations my tiny fingers had made.

Mum assured me that things would get better with time.

"It will be all right. Papa gets mad when he works hard and comes home to a dirty house," Mum said.

"I know dirty house does not look good."

"See, you understand. You are such a smart girl. Keep your pencils and notebooks in the right place after you have finished homework."

"Yes, Maa," I said as obediently as I could.

I thought our pain was transient, but it returned day after day, every day. I had never cried when I was in pre-school, but I cried every single day in kindergarten. Deep inside, I wanted to go back to my grandparents' house but I also wanted Mum. Even at that age, I knew it well that Mum needed me to be sane.

In a few weeks, I discovered a few hills about a quarter mile behind our house. They were thirty-forty feet tall. Some hills had wild flowers and mango trees, very unusual for a place like Rampur. I was completely fascinated by some of the wild plants on those hills.

A lot of the neighborhood kids played on those hills. They invented games, like climbing to the top and climbing down and collecting pebbles within a certain time frame.

I preferred going to the hills alone. One of my favorite things to do was to climb slowly while humming to myself. It gave me a thrill because when I was going up, all I wanted to do was to reach at the top. Once I was at the zenith, it felt good to see the ground. There was less noise and more peace. The view was great, and I loved the touch of wind on my face. The trucks on the roads carrying tons of coal looked tiny. It was the first time I found out that huge things looked small from a height and that discovery made me feel proud, because it was something that I learnt on my own.

I loved coming down slowly, step by step, humming again. I stopped to see the different shapes of rocks without touching them. There were many types of lady bugs under the stones. I could watch those little creatures for hours. I found nature, those hills, small wild flowers, and the tiny insects quite mesmerizing. I was fascinated to see how they crawled on their almost invisible legs.

I told Mum the stories about the things I found on the hills. She was my mother, my caretaker, my true admirer, my best friend, and my guide.

One evening in the month of September, it started to rain while I was trying to dig holes for the ladybugs. Hitherto, I was never allowed to get wet in the rain, but that day, I was all alone on top of a thirty-foot hill. I had a sudden yen to get drenched, and I did.

I was soaked with water when I entered the house. My father lost his temper completely and hit me hard on the head. I felt so dizzy that I had to sit down. That was the first time he had hit me that hard. I was shocked, confused, and totally terrified.

He kept saying, "Why did you get drenched? Didn't you know that you could get sick with cold wet hair?"

I cried my eyes out that night. I was so cowed by his anger that I was shivering when Mum came to the bedroom to tuck me in.

I told her, "I don't like staying here. I want to go back to Grandpa's house."

Mum stroked my head and said, "I know the beatings weren't good. I am really sorry about what happened. I will talk to your father."

She assured me that my safety was her first concern.

Mum continued, "You can't get drenched like that. But I am curious to know what were you doing up there? Didn't you want to come home when it started raining?"

I was so glad that Mum asked me what I liked there. Suddenly, I felt no pain, and there was a twinkle in my eyes, "I love the smell of rain. I love the sight of ladybugs. It is so much fun to get drenched, Maa. It was wonderful!"

Mum held me tight and cried that night. She kissed my forehead and stroked my hair once again as I drifted into my world of dreams and fantasies.

And life went on. Mum clung to the hope that someday everything would work out and we would be happy together. Hope—that was Mum's strength and she held on to that.

But that was also the tragedy; hoping for a change. "Hope" was never the problem actually. It could never be the problem, for it is the very foundation of human life. The problem was hoping for a change from the wrong person.

Chapter Four

Spring 1983, Kindergarten

As human beings, we all react to difficult situations in different ways. We all develop our own coping styles. Don't we? Some become aloof. Some become reticent. Some blame themselves. Some become hyper-sensitive. I was developing a personality of my own with all these facets combined.

My situation was unique. While I had my own emotional battle at home, I didn't find solace in school. In the kaleidoscope of life, I had no colors, only black, no matter what direction I looked. I did not like the school much. I also didn't like Rampur.

I was sick a lot, so got tired easily when I ran during recess. I was also a dreamer and often drifted away in my own thoughts. I made a mess when I ate food. On top of everything, I had a runny nose that refused to stop.

I was way too thin and lanky. I had short hair. Mum preferred it that way because she didn't want me to get a cold. I liked it, too. It was less work for me. In a strange way, I had no qualm about being the weirdest child. But in spite of all this, there was a silent confidence inside me. I was good in Math. One of my teachers often told me in school, "Lisa, you are so smart!" Needless to say, she became my favorite teacher.

I tried my best to cope in school. I managed to survive the long eight hours with my fragile health. But nothing really worked. I was constantly let down and felt dejected. Most girls had their own groups and knew each other for a long time. Probably because I wasn't that regular in school and I missed many days of school during winter months.

With time, it started to bother me. I hated waking up in the mornings. There were days when Mum had to drag me out of the bed to get me ready for school. It was around that time I discovered the thing that affects us the most; a sharp tongue! I could clearly see how words become the most powerful weapons in life. It cut my spirit in pieces.

One night, I broke down in front of Mum when she was putting oil on my hair, "I think I should have long hair."

"Why, sweetheart?"

"I don't know."

"Do you like long hair?"

I replied, "Not, really."

Mum asked again, "Answer me, honestly. Do you think you will be treated better if you have long hair?"

I thought for a second and then said, "I don't think so."

Mum assured me, "You know, at the end of the day, we all want to be accepted and loved. Each one of us. You are not an exception. But if acceptance comes with a price of changing your inner self and what mattered to you, then it is okay not to be accepted."

Mum's words worked like a balm to my tired mind and gave me the confidence I was looking for. I decided to change nothing about my appearance.

My favorite day of the week was Sunday. I had a routine for every Sunday that I loved. After doing my homework, I climbed to the top of the tallest hill behind our house. That was something I looked forward to.

With time, I started to enjoy my solitude, far from all the turmoil in my life. I could sit there for hours and let my restless mind wander in different paths without any purpose.

In my mind, I could play the games I wanted. I could be a princess in a castle. I could be friends with anyone I wanted. I loved the company of my thoughts. I had made a shield around my own little world. It protected my thoughts. They became my companions through thick and thin. I could punch the nasty people around me, I could stand up for myself, I could answer back to my father when I knew I had done nothing wrong; all in my thoughts though! But in reality, I had a long way to go. I was timid in front of my father. He scared me.

One weekend, my father got mad over some trivial stuff. I was so scared of him that when he came to hit me, I ran.

I ran as fast as I could and stopped only once. I reached at the top of the hill. I sat there for a long time. I was hungry, tired, and cold. Most of the houses in Rampur used earthen stoves those days and used coal as the fuel. I could see smoke coming out of the chimneys from a lot of houses and wondered what they were cooking. But the last thing I wanted to do was to go home.

I didn't realize when it became dark. I would have sat there the whole night, had my mum not come to fetch me. Mum and I walked home crying. When my father saw us, he was mad that I dared to run away.

He looked at me and said, "I will slap you so hard that your teeth will come out."

When he came to hit me again, Mum stood in front of me like a shield. I don't know why but he backed off.

That night, I wondered if he loved me at all, if he ever felt anything when he saw my face wistfully looking at him for a hug, if he ever felt anything when he saw the notes written by my tiny fingers.

His attitude remained the same; cold and indifferent for many days after that. My tears were the unspoken words waiting to be heard. It was almost impossible to measure the magnitude of hurt I felt that night. I couldn't sleep a wink.

January 1983, Rampur, Odisha, India

In January, Grandpa had called Mum and came to know that I was sick with high fever and enlarged tonsils. He took an overnight bus to come see me in Rampur, arriving at six in the morning when it was still dark. He waited anxiously for an hour, then got a taxi to come to our house.

My father wasn't very fond of my mum's side of the family, and his least favorite person was Grandpa. Whenever my father and Grandpa interacted, my father avoided making eye contact. If Grandpa asked him a question, my father would always answer in one or two words. There were times when he didn't answer at all. My father never asked about Grandpa's job or about my mum's siblings. I guess Grandpa knew those vibes, maybe that's why he seldom visited us in Rampur.

But this trip was an exception, he was coming only for me. When the taxi reached our house, I was sitting on the couch in the living room, covered from head to toe in a beautiful red blanket stitched by Mum. Fever and cough had kept me awake in the dawn.

Every morning, a big, blue truck came to dump coal in front of the houses, so the residents could use them for cooking. The truck had just left and Mum was bringing coal in buckets to start the earthen stove inside the house. Mum was pleasantly surprised to see the taxi when it arrived. When Mum saw Grandpa come out of it, she started crying with happiness.

"Dad, is that really you? I can't believe it," Mum said.

"Let me carry those buckets for you." he said.

Grandpa had no suitcase, just a black backpack, and followed Mum into our tiny one-bedroom house, carrying the heavy bucket filled with coal pieces.

"How is Lisa?" was his first question.

Before Mum could reply, I hugged him, overjoyed. He was the last person I was expecting in the early hours of the day.

"How are you doing, Lisa?" he asked again lovingly.

"She is okay. Winters are always hard on her, you know," Mum answered for me.

"I am fine," I said in a low voice.

Mum offered him a wooden chair in our tiny kitchen while she made tea. "Tell me about everyone. How is Maa doing? How many more years for your retirement, Dad?" Mum asked him so many questions at one go.

"Oh, your mother is fine. She misses you a lot. She has sent some sweets, your favorite ones," he said while taking them out from the backpack he was carrying.

I had no interest in food and sweets, I was just elated and content to be with him. He sipped his tea while stroking my forehead and I sat there listening to his conversation with Mum. There was always a special glow on his face when I sat by his side.

"Are you taking care of yourself, Nina? You have lost weight," he asked Mum with genuine concern on his wrinkled face.

I wasn't surprised even a tiny bit. Mum had become thin, her hair was unkempt, and there were conspicuous dark circles under her eyes. There was no sign of happiness on her face.

"Come on, Dad. You have become like Maa and you think I don't take care of myself. I am fine," Mum pretended as if everything was okay.

Soon, my father was up. He came to the kitchen asking loudly for his tea.

"Where the hell is my tea?" he shouted. He had no idea that Grandpa was sitting there. When Grandpa heard his voice, he held me a little tighter. Once my father saw him, his expression changed. He lowered his voice while his eyes reflected surprise, anger, and hatred.

"Oh, well. When did you come? We weren't expecting you. How are you?" he asked with little interest.

Even though my father's voice changed from loud to soft, Mum could sense instantaneously that his presence was inopportune. Her smile faded away the moment she saw my father.

As usual, he didn't make eye contact with Grandpa while asking questions. As I looked at my father's face, I saw a raging anger that could bring out the worst in him. I knew my father was unpredictable and as I sat there studying his face, I had only one prayer in my mind; for him not to flip.

"Oh, I came an hour back. Heard Lisa wasn't doing well, so thought of stopping by for a few hours," Grandpa said it in a very calm voice.

"Of course, I wanted to meet all of you, too. There is a bus at four-thirty in the evening today, so I plan to leave around three," he continued.

The way my father was sipping his hot tea made me so scared that I thought I was going to have a panic attack.

33

My father turned towards me and said sternly, "Go and brush your teeth. Do I have to remind you?"

I left without a word. I could still see Grandpa from the bathroom, his head hung low as he drank his tea.

My father sat there without saying a word. Grandpa tried talking to him once again. "So, how is work?" he asked.

"Work is good. Everything is good," my father said.

Grandpa understood that he wasn't interested in talking, so he left it at that and continued drinking his hot tea.

Sometime later, Mum made breakfast and we ate in total silence, something that was painfully strange. A type of quietness that could speak a million words. All we heard was the sound of the spoon on the plate and food being chewed in the mouth. But amidst all this, I was glad to be with Grandpa. His warm smile was all that I needed at that moment.

Half an hour after eating breakfast, I threw up. Mum ran to clean it up as soon as possible. My father sat there watching T.V., totally indifferent to what happened around him.

Mum changed my soiled clothes and asked me to take rest. I fell asleep almost immediately and when I woke up, it was almost time for Grandpa to leave.

"Please, Grandpa, stay back for a couple of days. I haven't spent any time with you at all. Please. Please. Just two days," I begged him.

I guess he wanted it, too, so he agreed. But I forgot we needed my father's permission for my grandpa to stay in our house. My father went out in the pretext of buying vegetables that night and didn't return until eight.

I was glad that I had the time and freedom to spend with Grandpa who listened to what I had to say. Physically, I was exhausted but that didn't stop me from laughing and telling him stories. We played a board game, laughed, and cuddled while Mum cooked dinner.

Mum was combing my hair while Grandpa talked, my father walked in.

"Go to bed now. I mean right now," he ordered me.

"Yes, sweetie," Grandpa said, "Go to bed. We will talk tomorrow morning."

Grandpa stayed with us for three days during that trip, his last trip to our house. He accompanied Mum and me to the doctor's appointments. As it turned out, I had a severe infection and was put on a high dose of antibiotics.

I especially loved dinner time with Grandpa. He never took a second serving of food, no matter how much he liked the dish. Once we were done eating, he asked me to make some sound or beats on the wooden table.

"This sounds funny," I found it hilarious.

"This is how *tabla* is played, Lisa," he explained.

"*Tabla*, what is that?"

I laughed out aloud as I found the name funny, too.

"*Tabla* is like playing drums but you play with your palm and fingers. Mostly, it is played on a wooden surface. It is a beautiful musical instrument."

"Did you ever play *tabla*, Grandpa?"

"Yes, little bit."

"I want to be *tabla* player when I grow up."

"You can be anything you want. I just want you to lead a normal, happy, and healthy life," Mum said as she took a break from reading newspaper and join our conversation.

"Did you ever play *tabla*, Grandpa?"

"Yes, I did, when I was in school. My brother used to play it and he taught me little bit."

That made me chuckle and we spent another one hour blissfully playing tabla.

Three days later, I felt better when I woke up in the morning. I was awake and was about to get up from the bed when I heard the conversation between Mum and Grandpa.

"If you ever need anything, let me know. Absolutely anything. I feel responsible for your arranged marriage. Call me if you need money and I will wire it," he said in a whispering voice as if he was trying not to wake me up.

"We are fine. Everything is fine, Dad. Trust me," Mum assured him in a cracking voice.

It became clear to me that Mum didn't want anyone to know about the troubles at home. That's how she always had been. She did not share her problems with anybody; she made every effort not to let even my grandparents know how bad things were in Rampur.

"I know Chaka does not like me much. But that's okay. I want to be sure you and Lisa are fine," Grandpa said quietly to Mum.

"We are fine, Dad. He treats us well. The doctors in the hospital know us, too. The neighbors are helpful. I can actually see our apartment from my classroom window. It is a small town and people here are very kind. Don't worry about us. You take care of your health, okay?" Mum repeated what she had said before.

When Mum came in to open the curtain in the bedroom, I pretended as if I was fast asleep. She took my temperature.

"I am so glad, your temperature is normal, Lismun," she said while folding the big blanket on the bed.

"Can I go to school today?" I asked while rubbing my eyes as the sunlight fell straight on my face.

"Are you sure you can handle eight hours in school?"

"Yes, I can."

I wasn't really sure if I wanted to go back to school but Grandpa was leaving in an hour or so and the last thing I wanted to do was to be home and miss him terribly.

My father left for work early in the morning. Mum helped me get ready for school and fed me a good breakfast while Grandpa packed my lunch and polished my black, school shoes.

Mum had requested a neighbor, I called him Singh uncle to drop off Grandpa at the bus station. Singh uncle was at our front door exactly at eight in the morning. It was hard for me to say bye to Grandpa, but I had to do it as it was time for school. Once Grandpa left, I headed towards my school bus stop. As I walked few steps, I realized I had left my water bottle at home. I ran back to grab it.

The front door of my house was ajar. I saw Mum crying loudly in the bedroom. I wanted to hug her tight, but I didn't. I walked quietly, picked up the water bottle, and ran fast. I hated tears in my mum's eyes but that was what I saw most of my childhood.

When I came back from school that evening, I saw my father watching T.V., his legs stretched on the coffee table and his back facing the front door of the house. He turned towards me, "Why did you have to tell your Grandpa to stay back?" He screamed at me while throwing his dirty pair of socks towards the window.

I was shocked that he would say such a thing and yet, I knew all too well his extreme anger that controlled all of us around him, the anger that created riots in our minds. His red eyes carried storms in them. I was scared to death because I was the reason.

"I am sorry, Papa. I wasn't feeling well, so asked Grandpa to stay back," I murmured in a very scared voice and with gooseflesh on my skin.

His rage was unassuaged by my apologies. Instead, it made him more furious. He kicked the wooden chair near the wall so hard that one of the legs broke.

He looked at my mum with utter disgust and said, "Your father stayed back in my house like a dog. Yes, your father is nothing but a dog."

Mum was way too shocked to say anything. She ran to the bedroom crying.

I felt there were dark clouds around me, and I was getting shrouded in them.

"I am so sorry, Papa. I am really sorry. Will you please forgive me?" I said while shivering. But he was in no mood.

I stood in one corner while he upbraided me for nearly three hours that night. My sobbing became desperate cries. By the end of it, I was so frightened that I cowered under the bed.

I felt suffocated, but I couldn't. The gut-wrenching screams from my soul were so loud that I felt deaf.

I assumed that because I was culpable, I deserved the admonishments and scolding. At the same time, I was baffled because I was being punished for spending three days with Grandpa, someone who loved me so selflessly. My heart ached to the very core that night. I felt guilty, sad, and angry.

But that is what it was. That is how our society operated. We lived in a society where we were told to hide the bones in the closets, so I assumed it was the right thing to do. And that's what I did, I never talked about what happened at home and hid all the abuse and pain under the blanket.

It was past midnight when Mum woke me up to feed me dinner. I promised to myself that I would never ask Grandpa to stay back with us no matter how much I missed him.

The next few days were pure hell; lots of verbal abuse. Once he got tired of abusing me, he went back to his stoical self. Then everything in the house became quiet. Nobody talked. But I was happy and relieved, because, to me, silence was gold and the last thing I wanted at that point was to hear was his voice.

Chapter Five

1983, First Grade

When Mum was pregnant with my brother, she developed anemia. Grandpa begged my father to let Mum stay with them for the delivery. My father agreed very grudgingly. It was a tough situation because I had started first grade in July and my school was in session. It was a new school, and I was still getting used to it. Mum's due date was in September and the only option was to leave me with my father.

One night, I heard my parents talking.

My father said, "I am really busy. I don't think I have the time to take care of Lisa."

"What do you mean you are busy?" Mum asked him in irritation, "You are going to spend time with your child. She is your daughter, and she loves you. It is never a wastage of time to be with your kid."

My father said in a rude voice, "It is my life and my choice. Don't tell me what to do."

He paused, then said, "Fine, I will take care of her."

Later that night, Mum asked me, "Lismun, do you want to come with me to Grandpa's house or you want to stay here for school? Think about it and tell me in a day or two. You have just started first grade. I don't want you to miss out on your studies."

I thought for a couple of days and told Mum, "I will stay here with Papa. I want to do well in school. You go."

That weekend Mum cleaned the whole house, did some shopping, and packed the kitchen cabinets with my favorite snacks. The night before she was about to leave, she sat on a chair. I rested my head on her lap.

She said softly while combing my hair, "You know, Lismun, I really like the type of person you are becoming. I trust you."

I asked her innocently, "Tell me, how you trust me."

"I trust you with my heart. I have this feeling from inside that you will take care of yourself in my absence. Avoid eating the foods that are not good for you. Sleep on time."

"Okay, Maa."

After Mum left, it was my father's job to get me ready for school. He hardly spoke to me and when he did, it was in monosyllables.

Even though Mum's absence was unbearable, I consoled myself thinking the separation was temporary. At the end of it, I was going to have a sibling to play with.

It was a bright Thursday morning in the first week of September. The weather was perfect. Thursdays were physical education days in my school and all students were required to wear white school uniform.

The day started off like any other typical day. I was awakened by my father, then I got ready by myself. I had been feeling a little tired and sick but decided to go to school. I had a piece of plain bread for breakfast, wore my white school uniform, and was out of house much before the school bus came.

Some of the girls were playing tag during recess that day. I liked a girl in my class, Anna. She was quiet and much calmer than the other girls. Anna invited me to play the game, I couldn't say "No". I hesitated for a few seconds but happily joined them after five minutes. I flashed my sweetest grin and ran to play. Somewhere in the middle of the game, I was pushed. I fell with my face down hard on the ground. My forehead hit a big stone and I cried in pain. It felt like my brain stopped working as I stood up. Blood was dripping and I froze. The girl who pushed me ran away from the scene as she got scared after seeing blood everywhere. But Anna helped me stand up and held my hand as we walked inside the school building.

I went to the restroom and washed my face over and over. When I looked at myself, I was horrified. I looked like a clown. There was a big bruise on my forehead from which blood was oozing out. I held the wound as tight as I could.

It was a mess and I wanted to stop my tears but could not. It was so painful that I felt I was going to faint and die. I held the wound, pressing my handkerchief against it for a long time. Eventually, the blood flow stopped. But there was blood everywhere, on my bangs, all over my white uniform. That sight of blood was terrifying to me and made me even more upset. Finally, I mustered the courage to walk back to the classroom.

My teacher was shocked to see me like that.

"Lisa, what happened? There is blood all over your forehead. And look at your clothes!" she said.

I wasn't sure if the push was intentional and moreover, I was apprehensive and heart broken. I didn't want to name anyone.

"I bumped against a rock and fell down," I said calmly.

"Tell me how can I help you? Do you want me to get some ice cubes?"

"No, I am fine. The bleeding has stopped. My mother has taught me that if you are ever bleeding, then you hold that spot tight or press it with cotton or something. I pressed it with a wet handkerchief and that stopped the bleeding."

"Okay, good. I am glad you did that. When you go home, change your clothes."

"Yes, ma'am." I replied.

My teacher dropped the matter there.

That evening, when I rode the bus back home, I looked out of the window the whole time. I missed Mum so much that day. But I carried a slight hope, somewhere deep inside me that I would be able to talk to my father.

All I wanted that night was to cry my heart out. But I was only naïve and foolish to think my father had any interest in talking to me.

As we ate dinner, my father didn't see my bloody forehead, tired face, big swollen eyes, and blood-stained clothes. I am not sure whether he failed to notice or he just ignored it altogether. I had never wanted a hug that bad in my entire life.

He was reading newspaper while eating food. He didn't care enough to look up and talk to me. I coughed a little to get his attention. When my father heard me coughing again, he said, "Drink few sips of your milk and go to bed as soon as possible. You have school tomorrow."

After dinner, I went to bed in the same school uniform with a traumatized soul and with a bruised heart. My little hands shivered a bit more as I wept helplessly and my red swollen eyes became so big that I couldn't keep them open. Then I sang a lullaby in my quivering voice to calm myself down and drifted away to deep sleep, far from brutal realities.

Next morning, when my father tried waking me up, I couldn't open my eyes. He tried again.

He said, "Lisa, wake up. It's time for you to go to school. If you are late, you will miss your school bus."

But I could hardly open my eyes and I felt so debilitated that I couldn't talk. Getting up from the bed was almost impossible. When my father touched my hands, I had high fever. Again, he said nothing, absolutely nothing. He dropped me off at my grandparents' house. When we reached there, Mum opened the front door. Grandpa was at work.

He said, "I can't take care of a sick child."

When my father dropped me off, I felt so overwhelmed with all the emotions pouring in from different directions in my little head that I felt dizzy. I was confused, defeated, shattered, but most of all, I was rejected. The feeling of rejection was so strong that I got totally engulfed in it. I closed my eyes tight as Mum held my hand and looked at my dirty clothes.

The last thing I wanted to see was my father's face. Mum was too shocked to react.

"Do you see her? Do you see her blood-stained clothes? What happened?" Mum cried while holding me tight.

"Don't know. Maybe she fell down. Ask her."

Mum stood there with me in complete shock while we watched my father leave.

1983, Sambalpur

That night was tough for both of us. We cuddled on the bed and Mum said, "Did he give you food when I was away?"

"Yes, he did. But I missed you, Maa."

"I missed you so much. You are my life," Mum said.

The way my father left me at my grandparents' house had a lasting impression on me. I often found myself crying when I thought about it. I was like a petal fallen from the flower. I thought my life was unfair and uncertain, and my wishes were unfulfilled and unattainable.

But it also made me strong in ways I did not even realize at that point of time. I was only six, but I was developing a determination that I was not even aware of! I was ready to grow wherever I was planted, and I was willing to thrive wherever I was thrown.

Being with Mum and my grandparents gave me strength. As crushing as my father's treatment of me was, their love lifted me up. I felt an invisible shield around that protected me big time from all the hurt hidden inside me. Mum made sure that I ate my breakfast, lunch, and dinner in time. Grandpa and Grandma never left me alone.

In 1983, my grandparents lived in Sambalpur, a big city in eastern India on the banks of Mahanadi River. They had their own house, and it looked like a palace. I loved its tall ceilings and big windows. The seven-bedroom house gave me a lot of room to run around.

It didn't take long for Grandpa to recognize my worries. He wanted to help and see me happy. So, every day, when he came back from work, he brought cake and fruit bread for me I ate the goodies while he drank tea. When we were done, he told me stories and we played games. I grew fond of that daily ritual during my stay in Sambalpur.

"Grandpa, I miss you when I am in Rampur. I miss my pre-school days in Balangir," I said while we were eating dinner.

"We miss you, too."

"So where did you go for pre-school?" I asked him.

"Oh dear. I didn't have that class."

He laughed.

"What? What was your first class then?"

I was curious to know more.

Grandpa carried me to the bed and put a blanket on me and said, "My school started with grade one. I didn't have a backpack but I had a plastic bag with a zipper. I kept all my books inside it. My school was on the other side of the river. I had to swim through it to get to school, so plastic bag was good. I swam the river twice a day for as long as I went to school."

"Swimming through the river to go to school! Was it fun?" I was way too surprised to even react to what he told me.

"Yes, most days, my friends and I had a good time in the water. But there were days when we were tired because the river was wide."

"Which river?"

"Mahanadi."

"I know, Grandpa. It is a long river, right?"

"Right."

"Grandpa, what did you do after school? Did you work?" I asked him again.

"After school, I went to college, Lisa."

"Hmmmmm…okay."

I started to yawn by then.

"I think you should go to bed now. You look sleepy."

"But tell me more about it tomorrow."

Next morning, we had a visitor from Bhubaneswar, Grandpa's friend. He was loving and talkative, just like Grandpa. I took an immediate liking to him and thought old people were very fascinating and genuinely good human beings. Grandma had made scrambled eggs for breakfast and a sweet dish made of up coconut and milk.

As I sat on Grandpa's lap and ate my breakfast, his friend said, "Lisa, do you know your grandpa and I started our first job together?"

"Is that why you both are friends?" I asked with food in my mouth.

"Yes," he said with a big grin.

"Do you know who was the first Prime minister of India?" Grandpa asked me as his friend took a bite of his breakfast.

"Yes, I know. Pandit Nehru," I said with pride.

"Very good, Lisa. Now I have another question for you. Do you know what is the longest dam in the world?" Grandpa asked again.

"No, I don't know."

"It is Hirakud Dam."

"Very close to Sambalpur," his friend added.

Grandpa continued as he fed me a spoon of scrambled egg, "When India got Independence in 1947, it started building Hirakud Dam. Yes, the longest dam in the whole world. I found a job in the dam project immediately after I finished college. Me and my team were actively involved in all the work. So, when Jawaharlal Nehru came to inaugurate Hirakud Dam in 1957, I got a chance to present him a rose flower."

"Can we go and see Hirakud Dam someday?"

"Yes, certainly. We will go soon."

Grandpa's friend stayed with us for three days and we spent a lot of time playing together. Grandpa was true to his words. We went for a picnic the next evening. The view of sunset far away on the other side of Mahanadi River bedazzled me. The skies had many dots and different shapes of pink, orange, burgundy red, and purple colors. The clouds and faint sunrays looked majestic. In twenty minutes or so, the sun was gone. Yet, it lit up the sky for some time. It was a beauty to appreciate and a miracle to marvel.

Spending time at my grandparents' house was all about making good memories and I loved every bit of it. When Mum and I were at my grandparents' house, Grandpa took me out for evening walks. He bought cupcakes for me while we walked.

One of those days, I decided to write my name on every single wall of the house. I was mischievous in that way and it was a secret nobody knew about.

Mum's older brother, Uncle Bhanja, caught me scribbling and drawing flowers on the living room walls.

"I know what you are up to," he said with a grin.

"No, you don't."

"You are writing your name on the walls and some scribbling, too. I saw you earlier but didn't say anything."

"I am sorry. This is the last wall," I had tears in my eyes and was scared that I was going to be punished.

"It's okay, don't say sorry. Go and write your name all over the house. Don't be scared," he gave me a pat on my back.

I thought my uncle was confused. I asked him in total astonishment, "Do you mean that?"

"Yes, this will be a secret between uncle and niece."

Uncle Bhanja kept his promise and did not say anyone about it. That day we became real good friends.

Chapter Six

My Baby Brother

My brother was born on September 16th, 1983. Mum named him "Joy." Unlike me, Joy was bony when he was a newborn baby. Mum thought one of his eyes was slightly smaller than the other, but to me, he looked perfect. I was so happy the day he came from the hospital. Having a little sibling meant so much to me. The moment I saw his little face, I knew he was going to be my best friend. He looked tiny and fragile. His delicate body supported his tiny head and I was worried if the edges of the pillow covers hurt him. When Mum asked me to hold him, I refused because I was scared that I was going to hurt his neck and head.

But I watched him from a distance. I was little frustrated because he slept most of the time. So, I waited patiently for him to open his eyes. When he was awake, I made funny faces to make him laugh. The thing that fascinated me the most was his smile in his sleep. That was the most captivating thing I had ever seen in my life.

I didn't feel any sibling rivalry with my baby brother. I felt love, lots of love towards him. I wanted him to grow faster and stronger, so he could play with me. I wanted him to talk to me and read books with me. In my little mind, I had a long list of things to do with him.

Ants Annoyed Me

One time, Mum put my little brother on the bed after giving him a nice bath. She had put coconut oil on his hair and he slept peacefully. I sat by his side drawing pictures on white paper sheets. I noticed he made weird faces while sleeping and he wasn't smiling. To me, it looked like he was in pain. When I went close to his tiny head, I saw lots of red ants. I cried out and ran to find Mum.

Mum was in the garden. I grabbed her hand and screamed in total distress, "Maa, come with me. Ants are eating the baby's head."

Mum ran inside the house and cleaned his head as fast she could. Soon, he went back to sleep.

That night, I asked Mum innocently, "Did the ants get into his brain?"

Mum laughed, "No, my dear. Ants were eating the sweet coconut oil on his hair. Ants didn't do anything to his head, your little brother is just fine."

I felt assured but I developed a strong aversion to ants for a long time after that day.

Grandpa's Stories

Grandpa was an expert in showing how great ordinary day to day life could be. He was a genius when it came to stories. He told me stories about ducks, swans, flowers, the raindrops on the flower petals, the morning dew on the grass, and the food my grandmother cooked. I listened to his stories in great awe.

I really enjoyed the witty stories of Akbar and Birbal. Akbar was one of the Mughal emperors and ruled India from 1556 to 1605. Birbal was a prominent advisor in Akbar's court.

My grandpa was a gentleman. If he was home and he was not telling me stories, then either he was helping Grandma in the kitchen or teaching the poor kids in the neighborhood who could not afford private tutors. He truly inspired me.

Back to Rampur

We returned to Rampur when my baby brother was one month old. My father was delighted to see him. Two days later, he bought a nice, yellow motor bike and took me for a ride.

"I love this, Papa," I said with sheer happiness on my face.

"I am very happy that you have a little brother. We can go for long rides in the evenings," he said.

Those were some of the happiest moments of my life. I couldn't have asked for more.

My favorite sweet those days was coconut cookie. I could eat that for breakfast, lunch, and dinner. There was a newlywed couple in our neighborhood. The wife loved to bake. So, it was a perfect situation; a little girl who loved cookies and a lady who loved to bake.

It became my daily ritual to go to their house and eat cookies. Of course, Mum didn't like it and she said, "You can't trouble her like that. She has other things to do. Next time, she offers you cookies, politely decline it."

"Why? She bakes it for me," I argued back.

"Yes, I know. That's why you need to stop. You can't trouble her. It is just not polite to go to her house and eat. I don't like it. Now, that's final," Mum said sternly.

"Yes, Maa," was all I could say.

One Sunday night, Mum and this wonderful lady were watching a movie and were discussing a recipe to cook together. I was sitting there, too, just blankly looking at the television. She had put a plate of cookies in front of us on the coffee table. Because Mum was there, I decided not to touch the cookies. Just then, we lost power and the room became dark. It was a perfect opportunity for me to grab the cookies and I did. Just when I was about to put them in my mouth, we got the power back and there was light in the room. Mum and this lady had a good laugh at my expense and needless to say, Mum let me eat to cookies because I had already embarrassed her a lot.

My father doted on my baby brother and took us out for dinner during weekends. We hardly ate out before that, so I looked forward to the new routine of eating out on Saturday nights.

One Saturday night, after coming back from dinner, Mum became emotional and hugged all three of us and said, "I am so happy. My world starts here and ends here."

I was curious to see what my father felt at that moment as I looked at his face. He smiled and he looked happy, too. Memories like those were pasted on the four walls of my mind forever.

At school, I kept to myself and didn't talk much. School was not great, but it was bearable. I had accepted the situation and had learnt to steer clear of any trouble. When I came home, I was a happy child to be with Mum and my baby brother. Life was peaceful for few months with little hiccups here and there.

When Mum went back to work, my father's mother came and stayed with us. She took care of my baby brother when Mum was away teaching in the school. It was a tiny apartment with just one bedroom. With an extra person in the house, it felt little crowded. But Mum never said a word against her and did what she was supposed to do; please everyone. There were constant demands for money and clothes, not just for my father's mother, but also for my father's siblings.

"You are the eldest in the family. You still have a brother in high school. You need to take care of siblings. You know we don't have a lot of money," my father's mother said one morning.

"Yes, Mother. That's why I earn money. I work hard, so my siblings can do well."

That made my father's mother happy.

One Saturday evening, when we got ready to go out for dinner, my father's mother said, "What are these dinner outings? All crap! Total waste of money."

"But I love going out to eat once a week," I said innocently.

She pretended she didn't hear me and screamed at my father, "You should be ashamed of yourself. You are wasting your hard-earned money eating food outside of the house. Why do you have to take your whole family for dinner every weekend? Once a year is fine. Your dad and I have struggled so hard to bring you up. You realize that, right? You have siblings to take care of. Do you ever think about their food, clothes, and education?"

My father canceled our outing that night. Not just that night but we never went out for dinner after that.

For all those months my father's mother stayed with us, there were unwarranted demands from her. Once, she told Mum point blank in front of me, "Ask your father to send money."

Mum did not say a word. When Mum got her salary for that month, she gave it to my father and his mother, every single penny.

As time passed, Mum became an epitome of patience and tolerance. No matter what my father said and how cruelly he behaved, Mum told me, "This is just a temporary phase, Lismun. Everything will be alright, everything will fall in place."

But things never changed, things never became alright. How could they when my father refused to change himself even a little bit. The sad part was that I was growing up and witnessing it around me.

As time passed, my father became verbally abusive towards all of us. He often lost his cool for small things, like a drop of sauce on the dining table or not being able to erase something from the paper. But Mum, somehow, found a way to make things normal by not answering back.

"When Papa is so nasty to you, why don't you say something, Maa? I don't like how he treats you," I asked her once with tears in my eyes.

"It's okay, Lismun. Don't worry about these small things. We live in a society that is male dominated. Your father makes most decisions in our lives. Nothing wrong with that. He was a very smart student in his time. There is so much you can learn from him," Mum told me.

As I grew older, I started to feel anger towards Mum. I didn't understand when she talked about the pressure from the conservative society or her logic about my father being brainy and bright. I didn't understand why Mum tried so hard to please him and tolerated the abuse. It never made sense to me because all I saw was the worst facet of my father's personality.

But in spite of all the odds and complete neglect from my father's side, Mum influenced me the most during my formative years. She had an unspoken confidence in me and I did strive hard to live up to it. She made me her top most priority and I always listened to her. In return, she surprised me by stitching beautiful dresses for me.

This was the paradox of my life; I received the maximum wrath and hatred at home from my father but received an abundance of love and affection from my mother. Under the same roof!

Chapter Seven

1984, Endless Expectations and Limitless Greed

My father's mother stayed with us for around three months. Once she left, Mum hired an eighteen-year-old girl, Banchi, as a nanny to take care of my brother. She was an orphan from a nearby village. When she started work at our place, she lived with us in our tiny apartment. As I didn't have many friends to play with, she quickly became my best friend.

Banchi taught me how to make tents with umbrellas. She said, "Let's put two umbrellas in front of each other and you see the magic."

"What magic?" I didn't know what she meant.

"That's your tent, Lisa," she said.

Few days later, my father's dad, who was a teacher, joined us. I called him "Jeje." It was almost eight in the night and I heard a knock on the door. When I opened the door, it was him.

"I had sent a letter few days back. I hope your parents got it. I will be here for one week. My school is closed because of some local strike, that's why I am here," Jeje said while making his way towards our tiny kitchen.

My father had gone out to meet one of his friends. We had finished dinner and Mum had cleaned all the cooking utensils and dishes.

"I haven't eaten any dinner," he said as Mum greeted him. He looked tired.

"Sure thing, I will make something for you now," Mum said.

Mum was right on target, making dinner for him at eight in the night. I don't know when Mum went to sleep that night and what time my father came home. Next day, we all ate breakfast together. My father looked happy to see his father and it was evident because he spoke only to Jeje while eating.

Jeje was nice to me and Joy and he never said anything to Mum either. But he always gave subtle hints to my father, "You have to talk to Nina about money. If she refuses, then you need to talk to your father-in-law directly."

I heard him telling my father many times when Mum wasn't home. I didn't like it that he spoke against Mum when she wasn't there. But the thing that hurt me the most was that my father didn't stand up for Mum.

In a couple of months, Banchi became a member of our family in our tiny apartment. Her morning routine was to walk with me to the bus stop. We both enjoyed it and talked on our way. One day, I noticed her face was sullen and she was quiet. It was unusual because she was quite a talker.

"Are you okay, Banchi?" I was really concerned for her.

"I am okay. Just thinking about life in general," she paused for a few seconds before saying, "I feel jealous of you sometimes."

"Why?"

"Not in a bad way," she said. "Look at you, you go to a good school, your parents have bought a uniform for you. I feel sad that I never had all these opportunities. It really matters where you are born," she said in a thoughtful voice.

By the time she finished her sentence, my bus had arrived. As I sat down on the window seat and waved at Banchi, I thought about what she said. I closed my eyes and thought for a second and even though I didn't have many things in life, I appreciated the fact that my parents sent me to a decent school and invested in my education.

I was instructed by my father to talk to his dad for an hour after coming from school, so he didn't feel bored. It really didn't matter how my day was or how tired I was. An order from my father was the ultimate command. I followed all his orders dutifully. So, this was also no exception.

One evening, Mum had just finished making dinner. It was mixed vegetables curry and rice, Jeje's favorite dish. I was sitting near him, telling about what happened in school that day. My father walked into the house when Mum was serving food. When he saw his dad eating rice and vegetable curry, he lost his temper.

"How dare you give such a simple dinner to my father? Can't you make any nice food for him? Just vegetables and rice? What type of dinner is that? He is our guest. Don't you understand it?" he shouted at Mum.

It scared the heck out of Joy and he started crying. My father's screaming continued for the whole evening. Once he was done, he ate his dinner and went to sleep in the living room. Mum, Joy, and me had no appetite that night. Mum held us together on both her sides and we went to sleep together.

Jeje stayed for another three weeks after that. Mum slogged from morning to late night every day during that time making elaborate meals. Mum's number one priority was to make good food for her father-in-law while Banchi took care of me and little Joy. I was just praying God to keep Mum healthy because she was working way too hard.

Banchi told me, "You know, Lisa, I don't like how your father treats your mother. When I get married, I will never let anyone treat me like that. I know

I am not educated but I don't care. If my husband treats me like that, I will leave him."

That was the first time I understood clearly that what we were going through at home was not normal. Unfortunately, nothing made my father happy. The harder Mum tried, the magnitude of his atrocities grew. He refused to acknowledge how hard Mum worked for all of us. Jeje kept adding fuel to the fire by saying something or the other to Mum.

"Oh, you could have made this curry little better. You know that rice you made, fried rice, it was little spicy for my taste," he said one afternoon after lunch.

I was sick of watching it. I always wondered what he achieved by it. But the one thing that really baffled me was the fact that my father enabled all this. Either he participated or he remained silent. That angered me, saddened me, and left me defeated. His love was a frozen thing and there was nothing I could do to thaw it.

If anything, my father grew angrier every passing day. And just within a year, we were back to where we were before my brother was born. There were many nights when I thought Banchi's life was better than mine, at least she didn't have a father like mine.

One day, when I came back from school, Mum was cutting vegetables. She was in pain because she had cut her fingers bad. My father's dad was watching television and Banchi was doing laundry.

Joy was playing on the floor and was in a cloth diaper. Mum was supposed to give him a bath, but she was busy cooking an elaborate dinner for her father-in-law. I offered to wash Joy. I don't think Mum heard it right. But I cleaned Joy, washed his face, hands, and legs, and put clean clothes on him. Mum couldn't believe it. I was just seven and half.

"You have done an amazing job, Lisa," she said with a proud grin on her face. I beamed with pride that evening. That compliment from her gave me a lot of confidence.

When Mum took Joy to feed dinner, I went behind her and said, "Will you leave Papa?"

Mum paused and turned back, "Why do you ask that question?"

"I don't know. I just feel he does not like us and we are not wanted here."

"Well, we are not going anywhere."

"Okay."

"No. It will be too hard for me to bring you both up all by myself. I am not that strong mentally. Besides, we have to be optimistic about everything in life. All problems can be solved with love and good behavior. I need to try harder."

My father remained indifferent for the next few days. He didn't speak a word to us. The silent treatment was something that we all found frustrating. It drove us crazy because we didn't know what his expectations were. Most of the time, he looked at us with total repugnance.

I said, "Papa, I am your daughter. Please tell me why you hate me?"

He turned to me and said, "I hate you because you love your mother and grandpa. Those are the two people I hate the most in the world."

He got up and slammed the door as he left home for that night.

I sat in that room with Mum, filled with the leftover feelings of anger and hopelessness and complete shock. Mum murmured to herself, "It's always a red flag when an adult man needs to be told to be nice to his kids."

Her face was blank and colorless.

When I asked if there was something, I could do to help her, she said, "Nothing. You are just a child. Your heart is delicate. You can't do anything. This is my problem and my fate, I need to take care of this. You see black as black and white as white."

I knew that I was intelligent, and my mind was agile. Mum knew it, too. But we were both stressed out, we were both upset. We both needed our personal space and sleep that night. So, we left things where they were and went to bed.

As days passed, I focused on my studies. We had a half yearly examination in December 1984. That kept my mind far away from being corrupted by family politics. My brain was free from the complexities of life, the darkness of the egocentric world, and the manipulations manifested by the relationships among people. I liked it that way. I stayed away from problems and problems stayed from me. The end result was great. I did well in all my subjects. That was another stepping stone for me to be more confident.

Jeje left after a few weeks. When Mum touched his feet, it meant she was asking for his blessings. But he said nothing, no word, no gesture, absolutely nothing, not even a mere goodbye. In return, I didn't say anything to him. I stood there and watched him go and thought about how ungrateful he was. The old man didn't even have to decency to bless his daughter-in-law or thank her for all the cooking and cleaning she did. He found his ego to be so big that he couldn't say few good words.

When I looked back, I saw Mum leaning against the blue front door of our house. I felt an undercurrent of anger and confusion. I didn't understand what Mum meant by society, I didn't understand why she tolerated so much non-sense. I thought all her logic about why she endured the abuse was severely flawed.

But the truth wasn't hidden from me. I could clearly see that in spite of all the odds and complete neglect from my father's side, Mum's courage remained unflinching, unwavering, undaunted, and unmatched. She was emotionally strong and maybe that's why she influenced me the most during my formative years.

It was true that home was where I learned all about determination, purposefulness, and resoluteness. Home was a place where my mum lived and to me, that was everything.

School Wasn't That Bad, 1985

By the time I started third grade, I had become stronger mentally and physically. My health was better with fewer sick days. My father hadn't changed at all, but I had found my own way of dealing with him. No matter how badly he belittled me, I didn't let him squash the reservoir of my inner strength. Maybe I found solace in Mum's company, maybe the years I spent with my grandparents as a little girl shielded me.

When my father's beatings, scolding, and snide remarks made me sad, I looked for things that made me genuinely happy; Mum and Joy. In spite of all my father's insanity, they helped me to bounce back to my true self; a happy and sweet child. I don't know what it was, but I had developed a weird confidence in my own self.

School was okay. I was doing well in academics and most teachers liked me. I liked my solitude and had my own imaginary friends. I talked to them, sang with them, and played with them. During recess, I walked behind a bush and talked to myself. A tinge of sadness shadowed my heart, but I didn't let it pull me down. I was happy and content just being myself. I think I enjoyed my own company most. There were days when I felt lonely but most days, it was manageable.

As I grew older, I made some friends, few girls in the classroom and in the neighborhood, too, but deep inside, I liked being a loner. I found it hard to trust people. I talked to them, studied with them, but didn't share my problems with them.

Initially, playing alone was my coping mechanism but it made me more confident. One of the girls in my class marveled at my ability of being alone.

She came and asked me, "How do you play alone? Don't you feel bad?"

I was puzzled for a second that she really wanted to know about me, so I started in a real gentle way, "My mum says it's okay to play alone. I am used to it now."

We were quiet for some time.

53

"What's your name?" I asked her.

"Pali."

"Nice name."

Pali thanked me and ran away to play in the sand. Pali was also one of those kids who also loved her solitude. A week later, she picked up a stick, just like I did, and asked if it she could play with me. We often played together after that. I was thankful.

Eventually I made quite a lot of friends in the school and the teachers loved me. It took some time, but school became more bearable.

Winter Vacation, 1985

By the end of 1985, I had developed slight tremors in my left hand, partly because of the fear I felt towards my father and partly because I was taking a medication for asthma, Tedral SA, which had theophylline in it. The tremors became worse day by day. Mum was preoccupied with my little brother and she knew I loved my grandparents, so she sent me to my grandparents' place in Christmas' holidays in December. I had ten days of winter vacation and to me, that was the best gift I could have asked for.

Uncle Bhanja lived close to my grandparents' house. I loved swinging by his place every day. He was a gem, a little eccentric though.

The most fascinating thing about him was his fearlessness. He had no qualms in telling people when he didn't agree. He walked out of his house during night time to enjoy the moonlight. He believed in his outlandish concepts and thoughts even when other people refused to believe it. I liked that fearlessness in him. He was honest and had the courage to speak what he felt in his heart of hearts. I admired his imperfection that he carried with so much confidence.

I told him once, "I don't like that long beard."

"Oh, really? But I love it. I look like a perfect professor."

I giggled.

"You know, Lisa. All professors wear glasses."

"Why?"

"Because they are absent-minded professors and glasses help them to find things that they keep here and there."

He was certainly someone I dearly loved. He was a math professor and a voracious reader. His wife, Aunt Lily, treated me well and took good care of me when I was at their place. One afternoon, we were enjoying the rain as we sat on the rocking chairs and sipped hot cocoa. Uncle Bhanja said while looking out of the window, "Lisa, can you tell me the meaning of philosophy?"

I looked at him and said, "No. What does it mean?"

"It means love for knowledge. 'Philo' means love and 'sophia' means knowledge."

"But what is it?" I asked him.

He said, "It is everything, let's say study of art, culture, existence, life. It includes anything and everything. A lot of it actually started with the Greek philosopher, Socrates. Socrates taught Plato, Plato taught Aristotle, and Aristotle taught Alexander, the Great."

I was just eight and I didn't understand anything he said but I liked listening to him.

Uncle Bhanja loved clothes and had several Nike shirts. One day, he looked really sad.

I asked him, "Is everything okay?"

He looked at me and said, "When I was coming back from work today evening, I saw a couple of beggars on the road. They didn't have any clothes to wear. I feel so sad."

"I feel sad when I see beggars, too. But what can we do?" I asked him.

He didn't say a word. He packed all his expensive shirts in a huge suitcase and donated them to the two beggars on the road. I was speechless.

Even though I loved his company, he annoyed me at times. One thing that bothered me was that he was a chain smoker. Smoking often triggered my asthma. Whenever I told him that I didn't like his smoking cigarettes, he stopped at once, only to start it a couple of hours later. At times, I felt he had no control over himself.

He taught me some basic concepts of math.

"Multiplication is nothing but repeated addition," he said once.

And another time, he said, "All even numbers are divisible by two."

"How do you find out whether a number is divisible by 3?" I asked.

"To find out whether a number is divisible by three. Look, here is the trick. If you have a number, let's say, 999, add all the digits and it is 27. So, 27 is divisible by 3, so 999 is divisible by 3, too. Let's say, 65. Well, if you add 6 and 5, it is 11. But 11 is not divisible by 3. So, 65 is not divisible by 3."

Mum's sister lived close by. I called her Aunt Renu. Her daughter, Litun, was Joy's age. We spent a lot of time playing together. They lived in an old house near Grandpa's house. It was a beautiful, green house and they lived in the first floor. The stairs were connected from the outside of the house. I loved the iron stair railing. Those were beautiful, carefree childhood days.

That Christmas vacation, I spent my free time doing math. Grandpa took me to a doctor who prescribed an albuterol inhaler. I liked the inhaler more than the medicine I had been taking. It was just few puffs and I felt alright. The tremors stopped when I reduced the intake of Tedral S.A. I did not feel weak inside. But more than anything else, I was just happy, being a kid, watching movies, eating what I wanted, and feeling loved.

Spring 1986

When I returned back home after spending some time with my grandparents and Uncle Bhanja, I wanted to score the highest marks in math. That's why I spent all my free time poring over math books once school started. I had become an expert in finding the greatest common factor, lowest common multiple, multiplication tables up to thirty, and big divisions.

My determination paid off. When we had our monthly tests in school that semester, I scored hundred out of hundred in every math test. That was a huge milestone in my academic life and made me more confident. As time passed, math became my favorite subject. When many students detested the subject, I excelled at it. My teacher challenged me with more difficult problems. I thrived.

Mum had more work at school as the number of students had increased considerably. Joy was two and half and was a little bundle of energy. He was all over the place and it took him just two seconds to make a huge mess. Mum was always running around trying to fix things. But being busy was good, it took her mind off from the problems my father created for us.

My health got better and I wanted to help Mum. She always made chai/Indian tea for herself when she came from work.

"How do you make this Indian tea?" I asked her one evening.

"Well, it's not very difficult," Mum said.

"Then teach me."

"No, not now. You are way too young. Maybe two years down the line."

"I want to learn now," I was adamant.

Mum was little hesitant but she finally taught me how to make the heavenly Indian chai.

She demonstrated while talking, "If you want to make two cups of chai, put one cup of water and one cup of milk. Let it boil for a minute, add tea powder, and let it boil for a few more minutes. Once it is done, it will have an orange color. The fragrance will fill the room. That's when you know your tea is done."

After making it with Mum for a few more times, I made it all by myself one evening. I poured water and milk and I let it boil. Then I added tea powder. It spilled out of the container when it was done. I cleaned the mess as much as

I could. I was so proud of myself. Mum was outside playing with Joy. When she came inside, I surprised her with chai.

"You made this, Lismun?" Mum asked.

"Yes, Maa."

Joy wanted to have tea, too. I looked at Mum.

"Can he have some, Maa?" I asked her in my sweetest voice.

"No, he can't. He is still a baby."

When Mum drank her tea, I saved mine. After Mum was done and went to take a shower, I put my finger in the tea and felt it with my touch. It had cooled down by then. I gave half of my tea to Joy. He loved it, the sugary tea, and I hugged him. He giggled and I giggled with him.

Making chai for Mum became a routine after that. We spent many evenings during the weekends, sitting around the earthen stove, burning coal, drinking tea, and talking to each other.

Chapter Eight

Absent from Home Summer, 1986

My academic year of third grade had been hectic, yet fulfilling. I had worked hard in spite of the domestic disturbances at home. I got an A in every subject, received the first prize in the handwriting competition in the whole elementary school, and accolades for my good behavior. But more importantly, I hadn't missed many days of school as I had fewer asthma attacks. I was happy with what I had achieved that year. After long, grueling terms and infinite class tests, we had the summer vacation. The one thing that I really looked forward to was getting up late in the mornings.

Mum's school and my school had the same last working day for that academic year. That evening, Mum asked me, "What do you want to do this summer vacation?"

"Sleep until ten in the morning and eat lots of good food every day."

"Oh, that's nice. We can do that. What would you like to eat?"

"Lots of French fries and cookies."

"Sure thing, sweetie," Mum said.

Mum kept her promise and pampered us with the yummiest food for the first two weeks. She made fries, cookies, different varieties of cakes, vegetable stir fries, and lots of jam from guava that we got from the two guava trees in our backyard.

I loved Joy dearly. His face was chubby, and he had a twinkle in his eyes. He loved running around, and I liked chasing him. I was glad I had summer vacation and there was more time to play with him. So far, my summer vacation had been good.

Apart from sleeping in, playing with Joy, and eating all the delish food Mum prepared, I liked drawing and climbing up the tall guava tree. Every day after lunch, I climbed up the tree with a backpack containing colored pencils, markers, white paper sheets, and some snacks.

Mum once commented I climbed up so fast that I looked like a little monkey. My preferred place was a branch on the right side of the tree because the view was great. I was thrilled to see three different streets from there when I looked in the north.

But my father had made a rule for me. I had to be home when he came back from work, normally around five in the evening. Knowing very well how he thrived on chaos and was uncomfortable when things were peaceful around the house, I made it a point to be home by four-thirty.

One morning, we all slept in, including Mum. When we woke up, it was almost nine and scorching hot. I wondered if my father had already left for work. I went to the front porch, then backyard, and then to the bathroom, but couldn't find him. But his office briefcase was still in the house, lying on the floor in one corner. His office shoes were still on the shoe shelf, shining. My intuition told me there was something amiss.

"Maa, wake up. I can't find Papa," I screamed near Mum. My heart raced fast and I thought I was going to have a panic attack.

"Sweetie, it is around nine in the morning. Papa must be in his office now," Mum said.

"His office bag is still at home, Maa."

"Let me call his office. If he needs the bag, maybe you can drop it off."

"Sure, Mum."

Mum called his office, but he wasn't in the office either. There was no note, no message, nothing. Mum had started to worry by then. She spent the next one hour calling people to find out where he was, but she got no information, no clue, nothing.

Joy and I were starving by then. Mum gave us milk and leftover cookies. There was no food in the house, except rice. Duty beckoned and Mum had to buy groceries.

"Take care of Joy. I will be back in an hour. I need to stop by at the bank to withdraw some cash," Mum was out of the front door even before finishing her sentence.

As far as leaving Joy with me was concerned, it wasn't unusual. Mum often left him with me when she had errands to run. So, like an obedient daughter, I did what she had asked me to do. I sat there with my baby brother and gave him my share of cookies, too. He looked confused. I read him some story books.

There was no credit card back then in that small town in India. People needed cash to buy things. Mum was frugal, so when she filled up the withdrawal slip in the bank, she wrote a small amount, just enough to buy the basic groceries.

"Ma'am, I am sorry. You have no money in your bank account," the bank teller said.

"What? What are you saying?" Mum asked, "Check it again."

She checked Mum's account again and said, "Yes, ma'am. You have no money in this account. Your bank balance is zero. Your husband, Mr. Bedbak, withdrew all the money from the account a couple of days back. I was the one who gave him the cash. He said he was going on some religious mission."

Mum returned home empty handed. When she entered the house, she held me tight and began to cry.

"Lismun, my head is spinning in all possible directions. I have no money, not even a meager amount to buy groceries. I feel dizzy when I think about it. I feel that someone is choking me."

I ran inside the kitchen to get her a glass of water. Mum spent an hour sobbing hysterically. She looked terrible as I wiped the sweat from her forehead.

"Please calm down, Maa. Tell me what else can I get for you. Talk to me, please," I pleaded.

"My mind and body are totally paralyzed. I am shocked. Your father has betrayed my trust."

"You need to tell me what is going on. I don't understand what you are saying," I had started crying by then, too.

"Lisa, we are penniless," she said while looking at the ceiling.

She drank all the water in one go.

"Can you get me more water, please?" she said.

My eyes were fixed on her face as she looked at fan spinning on the ceiling. I knew she was hurting, and as her daughter, it was unbearable. The pain in her eyes was so strong that it owned Mum and me.

Most of times in the past, Mum and I had managed to console ourselves. Not this time. My father's taking all the money from the joint bank account had jolted Mum from the core. It was so powerful that it swallowed every thought in her brain.

I did not have words to soothe Mum. As the clock in the kitchen ticked off the painful minutes, I felt a dull throb in my belly. It was because I hadn't eaten anything that morning.

Mum looked at me helplessly and continued crying, "How could he do that? Did he need money? Why didn't he tell me? Maybe because there is genuine problem. Where is he? What am I going to do now? How am I going to find him?"

She kept saying the same thing again and again.

I shook my head and looked into her eyes. Her panic irritated me and I almost screamed at her, "Stop this, Maa. What are we going to do now? You are the adult. Stop crying."

Mum put her hands on my shoulders and said, "We have no money. Your father took all the money out of our joint account. Our lives are over. We have no money to survive in this world."

I had gooseflesh all over my body.

"My monthly salary is so less. It took me nearly three years to save some money. I was intending to use that money for your education. But all that is gone now, just like that. The helplessness that I feel now is beyond any description. I don't know what to do."

Seeing Mum break down like that was a painful sight. I was devoid of words and couldn't say anything. At that point of time, I felt blank.

I just held her tight for some time and we both sobbed. We had plain rice and pickles for the next three days because there was nothing else.

But things grew worse. She'd never had a sleep problem and always slept like a baby. But that night, she was quiet, very quiet. She was lost in her thoughts. She said her mind was restive, there was no peace in the vicinity, and she needed more clarity.

When Mum tucked us in, she said, "I am worried about our future."

I didn't know what to say, so I just hugged her.

"You both go to sleep. I am going to make some tea and sit near the window. I need fresh air," she said.

There was a faint sound of a chair being dragged across the floor. The night was pitch dark and it was hard to see anything. It was the last thing I heard before my exhausted body went to sleep that night.

When I woke up in the morning, Mum was still sitting there. She was wide awake, but she looked tired. I put my arms around her lovingly.

"You okay, Maa?"

"I am okay," Mum said without even looking at me.

"When did you wake up?" I asked her.

"I don't know," she answered hesitantly.

"Did you hear anything about Papa?" I persisted.

Mum looked at me as if I was troubling her and she wasn't enjoying answering my questions. She took a deep breath before speaking.

"He didn't call yesterday night. I don't know. I have no idea where he is," she said in a dismissive tone.

"Did you spend your whole night sitting here?"

"I think so. I just couldn't move. I didn't know anything until dawn came. The sun rose slowly from the horizon today. Everything was so slow."

"Okay," I said, "I am hungry. Can we please eat something now?"

"Yes, go and brush your teeth. I will make tea and breakfast."

With great effort, she got up and made some tea. There was nothing in the house, no milk, no bread, and no vegetables. Mum made some black tea without milk and cereal for breakfast that morning.

I hated tea without milk, so I decided to remain hungry. A little later Mum took pity on me. Mum said, "Enough is enough. I am going to sell my silver ear rings to the neighbor." And she did for a small amount of money.

That day when Mum sold her jewelry was a painful one for us.

She took Joy and me for grocery shopping. With that meagre amount of money, she bought some basic stuff like vegetables, fruit, and milk. When we were coming back, Mum said, "This joint account concept will not work out."

"What joint account, Maa?"

"Having the same bank account with your father. He will withdraw all the money, even the money I earn."

I cleaned the house while Mum made lunch. She was exhausted and was severely sleep deprived. After lunch when Mum went to take a *siesta*, I ran out to play with the neighborhood kids on the streets. Mum didn't wake up until evening. It had rained a bit that afternoon and my feet were muddy.

When I returned home in the evening for dinner, I made the floor messy with my dirty shoes unintentionally. I knew I was in trouble. But I was pleasantly surprised when Mum didn't reprimand me for that.

"Go wash your hands, food is ready," she said in a calm voice.

Mum looked okay, if not perfect. I studied her face closely when we ate dinner that evening. She looked thoughtful but normal.

"I can take care of Joy if you want to go and search for Papa," I told her.

"No, I can't leave him with you. You are just eight."

"I can take care of Joy. Really, Mum."

"I told you my answer."

"Why don't you trust me?"

"I trust you, Lismun. But you are still a little girl yourself."

Mum hugged me and kissed me many times on my forehead.

I had another twenty, twenty-five days for school to reopen. A few days later, Grandpa came and took all of us with him. I was not sure if Mum had sent him a letter or telegram. In reality I couldn't care less. I was ecstatic. Joy and I had a good time that summer vacation.

Mum spent every afternoon making phone calls to find my father. The rest of her time she sewed clothes or knitted sweaters. Even though Mum was still worried about the money that disappeared, she seemed more at ease at my grandparents' house.

My grandparents' house was filled with our laughter and giggles. Joy was learning how to ride his small bike, Grandpa and I helped him. Those days were pure bliss, and every night, after dinner, we sat on the terrace of the house, telling each other stories. Joy and I were so busy that we hardly thought about our father.

But Mum did.

When it was time for us to go back to Rampur, I became paranoid. I hated the very thought of being there. I had started to wonder if my father had come back. But when we reached Rampur, my father still hadn't returned.

School started. I didn't talk about my father to anyone, nor did anyone ask. Mum was miserable at home because she still hadn't found out any news about my father. It was heartbreaking to see her like that. I always sat in the last seat of the school bus as it wound its way down the dusty streets of Rampur, past little houses, and the small vegetable market.

For me, there was no definite direction. Clarity was a distant dream. The vision was too blurry to make any sense. The more I tried to delve deeper, the more disappointed I became. The more I thought about my father taking the money, the more disappointed I became. I tried hard every day to block my thoughts from my mind as much as I could.

But her motherly instinct was always on guard. Mum saw my distress.

"You don't have to worry about anything. Yes, your father and I have problems, but they are ours. You don't have to think about these things. Your whole life is ahead of you. Make a future for yourself. You need to keep your focus on your studies and extracurricular activities," she said one evening when I came back from school.

I paid heed to what she said most times. I am glad I did. I went ahead and participated in activities, like debates, poetry recital, and sports. I had always liked reading poems, but I wasn't good at sports. Still it gave me a thrill and a new confidence that I tried.

One evening, when I had played a lot and my calf muscles were painful, Mum offered to massage them for me. As I sat on my favorite, yellow chair in the living room, Mum heated up some mustard oil to massage my bony legs.

I told her, "I like it when Daddy is not in the house. It just feels good. Let's go and stay with Grandpa and Grandma."

I didn't even blink my eyes while saying it.

It felt good to speak the truth. Like a big burden was lifted from my heart. I had thought Mum would slap me or something like that, but she was pretty calm.

She looked out of the window for few seconds, wiped her tears, and said, "Lismun, we live in India. This is a conservative society. I am never going to leave your father. You need to get it out of your head. This is his house, too; he will come back eventually. You know something, your father is not that bad. He was very bright, and he hadn't quite achieved what he was supposed to. That's why he gets frustrated at times."

"Why do you always call him bright? What do you mean by that? What's the point of education when he treats us like worthless creatures?" I was old enough to understand how much I disliked my father but I held Mum responsible. I didn't understand her reasons for taking crap from him. I was angry and frustrated.

"I am sure he will change with time. People change."

"I feel scared when he is around."

"I know sometimes he has a hard time controlling his anger. As long as I am here, you don't have to worry about anything."

"Can I stay with Grandpa and Grandma?"

"No, that can't happen. How will I live without you?"

"I can't live without you either, Mum."

"I am always there to love you, Lismun."

She kissed me on the forehead, "Go to bed now."

I was confused that night and spent a great deal of time tossing and turning. I was angry with Mum. I knew that she loved me, but I didn't understand what she meant by society and her hope that my father was going to change.

We got up early the next morning. Mum had already packed our lunch boxes. She announced that she was going to open three bank accounts; one for herself, one for Joy, and one for me.

"I am going to save every penny I earn. There is one thing that I want to make it clear. You both are going to have fewer sets of clothes and just two pairs of shoes, one for school and one for outside," she said with a determination on her face that scared the heck out of me.

Once we went to school, Mum did what she had told us. She went to the bank and opened three accounts.

My Father Came Back

It had been close to four months since my father was gone. Mum had not received any news from him at all. She had tried calling every single person in town, but it was futile. When Mum tried talking to my father's side of the family, it didn't help either as they refused to tell her anything.

My father's office promised that they would keep his job no matter what. He was good at what he did, and they sincerely hoped that he would be back soon.

I was nine and had started to understand my emotions a little bit better. I knew that Mum wanted her husband to come back. She prayed every single day for a miracle to happen. I loved Mum more than anything else and wanted her to be happy. I also realized that Mum needed more money for our daily expenses, so I prayed secretly when nobody was watching.

Meanwhile, to make ends meet, Mum offered to teach the neighbor's kids every alternate day. They agreed to it happily.

We celebrated Joy's third birthday at home, just the three of us, with blessings from Mum, some home-cooked food, vegetable curry, and rice. There was no fancy party, but Mum baked a nice cake. I remember it vividly because I didn't like the lunch that day. I wanted Mum to make a non-vegetarian dinner, but she had prepared a vegetarian one.

"I don't want to eat this food. Why can't you make something special even on Joy's birthday?"

"This is all I could do, Lismun," Mum was in no mood to argue with me.

"I don't want to eat," I said in an obstinate manner.

I remained hungry the whole day. I was hoping that like most days, Mum would come and coax me, but she didn't. I had to let go of my stubbornness next morning during breakfast as the hunger pangs had taken a toll on me.

One week later, towards the end of September, I made a huge fuss about food again.

"I want chicken. Nothing else," I declared.

"Don't show me that attitude. Do you remember what I told you about saving money? I don't have money for fancy food."

"Fine. Do what you want. I am not touching that food. Why do you always talk about money even for small things. I am tired of eating the same plain food every single day!" I screamed.

"Fine, I will make some chicken next week," Mum said, then left me alone.

Most of the time, I listened to Mum without making fuss and did what she told me do. But I absolutely didn't like eating vegetables and that's what Mum often cooked. So, I became stubborn when it came to food. I had become picky. If I didn't have my favorite food on the table, I preferred to be hungry. That frustrated Mum.

It was a cold Sunday night in November and I was happy. Joy and I had been good kids and hadn't troubled Mum at all. That's why she had made an elaborate dinner for us; mashed potatoes, bread, and chicken soup. I liked watching the weekly general knowledge quiz program on television during dinnertime.

I sat in the corner of the room, listening to the questions attentively, 'What year Gandhi was thrown out of the train in South Africa?'

The doorbell rang, and I ran to open it. There he was; my father. It took me a few moments to recognize him. He looked terrible. He had a long beard, unkempt hair, and dirty, smelly clothes. He looked like he hadn't showered for days. He had lost weight. It was the first time, I didn't feel scared to see him. I felt pity for him.

"Hello, Papa," was all that I could say.

He didn't say a word and went straight to the bedroom to sleep. My warm smile turned into a glum face.

Mum followed him but he didn't talk to her either. That night, for the first time in my life, I realized that as a child, I inherently loved my father. I was happy to have him home.

Mum had prayed every single day for him to return. Abuse was something I saw from a very young age, yet I loved my father. Yes, true, I loved the person who abused Mum, me, and little Joy!

But clearly, my feet weren't rooted in reality. Far from it actually. He remained cold and indifferent to all of us. Mum was relieved when he went back to work. For the first few days, he spent all his free time sleeping. He told us he was severely sleep deprived, but he still hadn't told us where he had disappeared for months.

A few days later, my father hired some people to build a small room near the kitchen. When Mum asked what was it for, he said it was a place for meditation. I loved the room when it was done. It had pictures of all the Hindu Gods. There was a worn-out, red rug on the floor. There was a mat to sit and pray. There were some white chalk pieces inside a box in one corner.

Everything changed after the room was built. My father had established a routine for himself. He got up early in the morning, took his shower, cleaned that tiny room, and spent hours chanting mantras for the Gods. When he came out after meditating, he looked content. Deep down, I liked it because his focus had shifted from us. I found it to be the most liberating thing in my life.

But he refused to tell us what he was up to. For the next three months, he didn't contribute anything towards the household expenses while Mum struggled to feed four mouths. She had to take care of our books, house expenses, food, and other miscellaneous expenses with her meager salary. We had no idea what my father was doing with his salary. Money was always so tight that Mum sometimes cried before making meals. It was heartbreaking for me to watch Mum go through that.

After waiting for months, Mum confronted him.

"Why aren't you contributing towards food and other expenses?"

"Because I am saving all my money," he said calmly.

"Saving for what? For the kids?" Mum was flabbergasted.

"No, I am saving for my spiritual journey."

"What spiritual journey?"

"I don't have to tell you everything," his sudden, loud scream terrified me.

"You have to. Wait a minute! Is that where you were?"

"Yes."

"You have to tell me about it," Mum looked angry and was crying profusely.

"I don't want to talk about it."

"You have to. You took all the money from our joint account. You have a responsibility towards us. I am an elementary school teacher, and I don't get my salary regularly. You know how the government works here. I get paid once in three-four months. We depend on you financially. Please tell us where you were."

"No."

"Why are you like this? Why are you so heartless?"

"I am not heartless. My priorities have changed. There is a spiritual path that will take me to God. I spent the last four months living in a house where they practiced all different types of meditation, the highest form of spiritual journey. Relief from the worldly pain!"

Mum put her hands on her head and sat down quietly on a chair. She refused to get up when I asked her to tuck me in. She didn't cry or anything; she just looked melancholic.

I went to bed early that night. My heart was pounding so fast from all the noise in the house that I thought I was going to have a panic attack. I promised myself silently never to make fuss about food again or any unnecessary demands for that matter.

The following days solidified what my father had said earlier. When he was at home, he spent his time in that tiny room. Out of the three of us, he treated my brother okay. My father seemed happy when he played with Joy once in a while. Even though he didn't contribute a penny towards the household expenses, Mum looked genuinely happy when he spent time with my brother. But it didn't last long.

One night, he finished his meditation and came out of his tiny room and got angry because of a trivial thing. The roof above his *puja* room was leaking. All hell broke loose after that and he refused to eat at home.

"We can ask someone to come and fix it tomorrow," Mum was begging him to stop.

He was explosive and used swear words. He started breaking the furniture with a thick wooden rod. His red eyes terrorized us. Joy and I stood in one corner watching his rage.

But Mum was the subservient wife, she wasn't going to give up so easily. She tried talking to him again. She pleaded with him again. But all she got was caustic remarks.

Next morning, when Mum went to the local market to buy vegetables, I offered to carry the bags for her. An old man who ran a coconut shop, a few blocks from our house had the sweetest ones. That evening, we stopped by to get some coconut water. I saw Mum taking out coins from her red, worn out purse that she had been using since I could remember.

"It's okay, Maa, we both can share one," I said with moist eyes.

"No, it's fine. I was just checking how old these coins are."

"Okay."

I knew that Mum was counting money, but I left it at that. There was an awkward silence between both of us as we finished our drinks.

That night, when Mum sat down on my bed, I asked her, "Papa seems to be so mad all the time. Is there anything we can do to make him happy?"

Mum said, "I don't know. He seems to have a lot of anger and hatred inside. He can't be happy if he hates himself."

She sounded so philosophical that I didn't know what to say.

Mum continued, "You know snakes shed their skin and develop new skin. I hope someday he sheds his skin of bitterness. I hope he confides his fears and apprehensions. It will be nice if we can start all over again, like the first rain of the season."

Dowry

I was never sure why my father disliked us so much. Dowry was still rampant in the Indian society in the 80s. My maternal grandparents were well off and my father expected Mum to get money from her parents.

Dowry was not acceptable to Mum. She always stood her ground and told my father straight to his face, "I am working. We both have jobs and our total income is sufficient for the four of us. I am not bringing dowry from my father."

As I grew older and learned about the dowry system in social studies at school, I asked Mum, "This system for girls to bring money from their parents is so old, it's outdated. Why does Papa expect Grandpa to send money for you, Maa?"

Mum smiled at me and said, "Greed".

It was true. Like money had tentacles. The grip was so strong that it destroyed everything, integrity, honesty, and ethics. Girls were burned alive because their fathers couldn't send money. Yes, educated women suffered, too, and my Mum was not an exception

But my mum was one tough cookie. No matter how many times my father asked, Mum never complied with it. It always did lead to nasty fights at home but she did not budge, not even when my father's parents put pressure on him about money.

She said defiantly, "I am not going to ask my father for monetary help, not even when God tells me."

My adulation towards Mum increased by a hundredfold because she stood for what was morally right.

It always surprised me because my father's younger brother was protective about his wife. One time, during a family gathering, when my father's Mom tried insulting my uncle's wife, he stood up for her and said firmly, "My wife is my equal and if you don't respect her, I will never see you."

My father stood there and didn't say a word. I studied his face closely as he sat in one corner, eating his meal, looking at the floor. I wondered what he thought at that moment because he never stood up for Mum.

Nobody from my father's side of the family talked to my aunt rudely after that day.

Then there were times when Mum and I felt my father's anger was not normal. His wrath terrorized us and made our flesh creep. The worst part was that we didn't know what was going to trigger his anger. Mum had tried talking to him in a calm way about anger management and opening up to a psychiatrist but those conversations ended badly. So, that chapter got closed and she never broached that topic again.

Sometimes Mum said, "You know, he is very frustrated because he couldn't achieve what he wanted in life."

I could never figure out what was the reason behind his indifference and cold attitude towards us. Maybe he was genuinely upset how his life turned out and took it out on us. Maybe, there were other reasons. But it really didn't matter why he behaved that way. As a child, what really mattered to me was that he hurt us, and he hurt us badly.

Finding Inspiration

During the days when I lived in Rampur with my parents, I made it a habit of reading newspaper every morning and there was a reason for it. I am not quite sure if I understood politics, national news or the entertainment pages very well as a young kid, but I discovered something about myself. I found that I was naturally drawn to people who struggled in life and came out of adversities on their own. I looked for those stories in the newspaper every morning. Most days I did find a story or two like that and reading about other people and how they overcame their problems and obstacles gave me an adrenaline rush. I thought that to fail, to fall, to falter and doing things all over again was actually about courage. A lot of courage. I remember being pulled towards that courage. I felt having that inner reservoir of courage to fight for yourself and for your dreams was the coolest thing and the biggest blessing one could ever ask for.

I was very fond of Anna and respected her from the core of my heart. She lived with her parents. Her mom had polio and her father was a loader. Both her parents were illiterate and didn't know how to read or write a single word, not even their names. But Anna was good at studies. I looked at her with awe. There was nobody to guide her but she did well in school because she was driven from inside. That amazed me. That determination. That power. That will. That strength. That focus. That personality.

I wondered if the gloomy coal mining town made her sad too. But she was always happy, always. I think after Mum, she was my biggest inspiration. Now when I am an adult and I look back, I have to say, there were many days when I dragged myself out of the bed to go to school just to look at her face.

Her calmness amazed me and baffled me at the same time. When most of the kids my age felt embarrassed to be with their parents, she felt proud when she stood near her parents during school annual functions. I loved and admired that facet of her personality. I loved being with Mum too unlike many girls. So we were alike in some ways. Unfortunately, Anna's house was far from my house and I never got an opportunity to meet her after school.

We were good friends, and I respected her a lot. I am not quite sure what she felt about me. Deep inside I longed to have the same courage that she carried. Her presence gave me strength in the class.

My Father Disappeared Again

At home, our situation remained the same. No change. Mum often spoke to me like an adult, as if I were her best friend. No matter how difficult our situation was. Fortunately, most of the time, I understood what she said. Sometimes, when I had a hard time processing some of the grown-up issues, I just nodded my head.

But Mum's wishes remained just mere wishes in a deep dungeon of her soul. They could never come out to see the broad daylight. Just like untold stories and unspoken words, the wishes died without becoming realities. A couple of months later, my father was gone again.

Mum and I felt like there was a wall and it was impassable. We had started to wonder if he was hiding something. We weren't sure about anything. The same cycle repeated; Mum called all his friends and relatives, asking if they knew anything about his whereabouts.

Mum left us at a friend's place and visited my father's parents for a couple of days. When she returned, she told me they had no information about him.

While Mum took the world in her stride and fought back fiercely everything that came on her way, she never asked anyone for money or for any help. Not even from my grandparents. She kept her self-respect on a lofty pedestal. She was truly my role model and she was the best mother in the whole world a child could have ever asked for.

"Out of the handful of things that are worth fighting for, the most important one is your *dignity*," was Mum's important message to me and Joy throughout our childhood days.

Working during the day, running around in the evenings to find information about my father and taking care of us in the night eventually took a toll on her health. I could see how fragile Mum had become. She looked extremely tired. She had dark circles under her eyes and her skin looked pale.

One morning Mum couldn't get up from her bed. I told her to stay at home and sleep. I promised her I would take care of Joy and I meant it. But Mum dragged herself to work. When she came back, she had a very high fever and severe body ache. She went to bed and couldn't wake up to make dinner for us.

I had spent a great deal of time doing my homework in the kitchen while Mum cooked. I had seen how she lit the earthen stove.

Now when she was sick, it was my turn to cook. I sat down with Joy and boiled noodles with some spices. Surprisingly, I didn't burn my fingers. Food was edible and we ate like gluttons. I was so proud of myself that night. For a welcome change, I cried, not because I was sad, but because I could cook a dinner for us. I was only nine, and that to me was an achievement in itself!

Next day, Mum felt good. When she was out of the bathroom, there I was with a hot cup of tea holding triumphantly for her.

As Mum struggled to make ends meet with her low salary, she remained calm. Outside our home, she walked with her head held high. She didn't ask for help, not even to Grandpa and Grandma. Keeping one's dignity on top of everything was the most important thing. She taught me.

The most amazing thing was that she was not bitter, not even a tiny bit. That was the foundation of her life; to be happy no matter what.

One evening, as we sat together outside our house, holding each other's hand watching Joy ride his tricycle, Mum asked me in a whispering voice, "Have you thought about your future?"

"No, I haven't. What's there to think, Maa? I am still a kid."

"If you haven't started, then you should now."

"Start what?"

"Plan a future for yourself. Do you want to live here forever in this coal mining town? There isn't a decent hospital here. There is no good school here."

"I agree with you."

"Lismun, I am not talking about Rampur or any particular place. I am talking in general. You need to be financially independent. You should have money to live life, not like me where I am counting coins before buying coconut water."

We looked at each other.

Mum continued, "You need a plan for your future. I don't want you to be stuck here in Rampur with the rigors of life, the miseries of painful words, countless sleepless nights, wondering why your father did this and that. Lismun, look for the bigger picture."

"What do you mean by that, Maa?"

"We are in a tough situation. We have nobody to help you out. You will have to figure out a way to help yourself."

"What do I have to figure out, Maa?"

"Your life, your future."

As time passed, Mum became a force to reckon with. She got up early, made breakfast for us, packed our lunch boxes including hers. Joy went to a play school where they taught him numbers and alphabets. We three left home around eight-thirty every morning.

I was in awe of Mum's way of handling money. Being frugal in our daily lives became her biggest strength. Every weekend, she sat down with us and made a budget meticulously. If we wanted something or genuinely needed any particular item, she told us to be precise about it. She had no money for our wants, but she managed to buy everything Joy and I needed.

Mum's dogged determination to face problems head on inspired me every single day. It made it easier for me to handle the situations.

At home, Mum told me every day to use my pain as a motivation to do well in school. She became an absolute rock for me. She made me feel that tears were transitory, like most difficult things in life.

She often said, "Greet each morning with a smile. A happy face is like a cleansing gush of water that washes away the dirt."

As a result, we stopped talking about the problems we had, but focused on our short term and long-term goals. We were a team; us against the world.

When my father disappeared for the second time, the blistering pain came gushing in again. But this time, Mum calmed herself in just a couple of days. She remained unperturbed and that made things uncomplicated. She didn't cry at all, even though she continued looking for my father. Sometimes, Mum acted like a robot, one job after another. Sometimes, we laughed about it, too. I called her the superwoman robot!

We just didn't talk much about my father and his absence. There was less stress at home as there was no shouting and no fights. I knew it well by then that Mum was the only person I could really depend on emotionally and vice versa.

I wore a smile around her, partly because I knew my happy face gave Mum a lot of strength, and partly because I wanted to think beyond my father and the problems in my life. No matter what, I had a silent belief in Mum that she would figure out strategies to deal with the problems in our lives, just the way she had always done. After all, she was the superwoman robot!

One afternoon, when she saw me running happily in a nearby park, she stroked my hair and said, "Keep smiling. Your courage gives me strength, my little one."

I looked into her eyes and told her with all sincerity, "Your strength makes me strong. We will be fine, Maa."

I was expected to take care of Joy during the evenings when Mum spent a couple of hours talking on the phone. She wanted to get to the root of the problem and wanted to find out the details about the spiritual journey my father was involved in.

A week later, my father's brother came to our house and told us everything about it.

"Well, there is this saint. She claims that she has seen God. She must be in her fifties and has quite a number of disciples. They meet every day and chant *mantras*. I know it is all fake and I can't believe that my brother fell for it."

Initially, Mum and I had doubts about it as he had never helped us out in the past. But he assured us that his intentions were clear.

"Look, I sincerely want to help you guys. It makes me sad to see how he is destroying his life," he said.

That night, Mum sat on my bed for a long time.

She said, "I think I should go and see what's going on there. I am not clear about anything. But there is no harm if I go and meet the saint, too."

"I will come with you, Maa."

"No, you are too young. I can't take you with me."

"Nope, you have to take me."

I refused to stay back and was adamant about going with Mum. I had an inkling that the saint was fake and my deepest fear was if they were going to harm Mum. She was left with no choice but to take Joy and me with her.

We left Rampur on a Saturday morning and boarded the earliest bus to Rengali, the small town where my father was staying. I sat on the window seat. Joy sat between me and Mum. I liked the rays of sun beaming through the trees and falling on my skin. It was bright and warm. I wanted to be oblivious to everything else.

Mum and I didn't talk during the entire journey, but Joy talked about superheroes and a wrestling match that he had watched on T.V. the night before. I wasn't sure how Mum felt. She was quiet. It was not unusual; she preferred talking less most of the time anyways. But I felt anxious and my anxiety crippled me. My gregarious self had become a thoughtful one.

I wondered what the saint looked like. Even though my little mind was mostly occupied with apprehensions, confusions, and the fear of unknown, I was also curious to know more about the spiritual path my father had taken.

Once we reached the bus stop in Rengali, we walked nearly half a mile through the town. There was a narrow stream of river and the road we walked on was on the side of the water. The cool breeze felt good on our tired faces. Finally, we came to the ashram, where this "saint" lived.

There were some railway tracks in front of the main gate. Just when Mum was about to open it, Joy saw a passenger train coming from the other direction. It was a weird looking train with different colored compartments. I didn't understand why it was like that.

Joy wasn't interested to see what was inside the gate of that *ashram*. There was nothing but sheer happiness on his face as he waved at the people inside the train. Joy kept waving at them until the sound of the engine was barely audible.

Mum opened the gate nervously and we went in with pounding hearts. It looked like some exotic hill station from British colonial days. There were some seven buildings scattered all around two acres of land. The whole area was surrounded by a fence.

I saw a huge vegetable garden on one side and a well on the other side. An old man, who was fetching water from it with a rope, smiled at Joy. I gestured to my little brother not to smile back at strangers.

There were lots of marigold and rose plants. They were all lined up in neat straight rows. One of the buildings was particularly big and beautiful. It was the only yellow building in the whole campus and was surrounded by fruit and flower plants. There were tons of small pomegranate trees, most of them were bent down because of the weight of the fruits.

Immediately, a couple greeted us warmly.

"Oh, Hello! Are you looking for someone?" the wife asked.

"We are here to meet my husband, Mr. Bedbak," Mum replied.

"Yeah, he is here."

The husband picked up some grocery bags and said, "Mr. Bedbak is such an asset to this *ashram*. Nice to meet his family. Well, I am little busy right now but we will talk in the evening."

"Sure," Mum said.

"Do you see that small building towards the end of the fence? It has only one room. That's the kitchen. It is nice to have the cooking place separate from other stuff. You know what I mean."

"I guess."

"Food is pristine. You have to watch what you eat. Food nurtures your body and soul. It is important what you put in your mouth. When food is important, then kitchen is important, too. We always cook fresh food here. Every single day. Every single meal. Everything from scratch. We have many varieties of vegetables here in the garden. Rice and spices, I buy from a nearby market. That's my job. Health is wealth you know. In case you are wondering who we are... Well, my wife and I are locals here. We don't have kids, so we come to the *ashram* every day to pray God."

I was mighty impressed to hear him talk about food and kitchen. But Mum didn't look interested in what he was saying.

"Okay, nice meeting you both. Do you think you can take us to Mr. Bedbak?" Mum asked.

"Yes, I will take you guys. Come with me," his wife said with a friendly smile.

As we walked towards one of the white buildings, I saw my father near a marigold plant. His facial expression changed when he saw us, more like he didn't like what he was seeing. He pretended as if he didn't know us and within minutes, he disappeared.

The lady who brought us there was taken aback, too, "I think he does not want to see his family here. I am not sure why, maybe he does not want to be disturbed."

"Does not want to be disturbed, what do you mean by that?" Mum asked.

"Oh, maybe you don't know about this. He is writing a book to make our saint famous."

"Writing a book? About what? What did you say?" Mum asked with a slightly angry face.

"He is writing a book about this place, about God, about the journey that relieves pain and sufferings. About the serenity of life here, calmness of nature, you know? All that stuff. I don't know how to say. He is the one writing the book, so he will be able to explain it better. Oh, I almost forgot, this building is for guests. Please go inside, someone will show you the guest room."

She was gone even before Mum could say anything.

To me, all these things were surreal. Too many things happening too fast. We stayed there for nearly six days. My father hardly spoke to us during that time.

There were around nine men and some twelve women in the *ashram*. Joy and I were the only kids. There was so much open space that initially it was overwhelming for us. But after a few hours, it was all ours. We ran all day, played in the fields, and ate lots of pomegranate. It was pure fun and very refreshing.

Mum washed our hands and legs every night before going to bed. But I didn't shower during our stay there for six days. I think Mum forgot about it and I didn't want to remind her. I was just happy running around and being dirty. I had nothing to do except eat delicious food.

My father was highly respected in the *ashram* as he was an intellectual and he was doing the herculean task of writing a book on them. They gave us a separate room to sleep in the night. There was no bed, no mattress, just a few mats made of up bamboo sticks. Mum asked them for some thin comforters and they happily provided us two floral blankets. I don't know how Mum felt about sleeping on the floor, but I had no problem with it at all. I was so exhausted during bedtime that I slept like a log. My father slept with us in the same room but he hardly spoke a word. He was lost in his own thoughts and didn't have much to say. Mum was quiet, too, and didn't initiate conversation with him.

I loved the food there. It was spicy and very tasty. Towards the end of our stay, I think, on the fifth day, my father took us to meet the saint. Her spacious room was in that beautiful, yellow building. We were told that she never came out of it.

The first thing I noticed inside her room was a big iron box. It was in front of the convertible bed where she was seated. She wore a yellow saree and sat on the tiger's skin. Her hair was really long. My father told us that she had never cut her hair.

As I wondered what that box was about, my father whispered in my mum's ears, "Put some money in the box."

Mum's face clearly showed that she didn't like being there. She still put some coins inside the box. I could see anger, frustration, and sadness all at the same time on the saint's face. She was so rattled because Mum offered her coins that she started stroking the tiger skin mat in a funny way. I found it too hilarious and started laughing. My father tried to salvage the situation and put a thick bunch of one hundred rupees notes in the box.

As the saint smiled, Mum's eyes were filled with tears.

That evening, Mum told me, "We are leaving tomorrow early morning. We will take the first bus that goes to Rampur,"

"Why Mum? I sort of like it being here. There is so much space to run around. I love it here. Let's stay here for a few more days, Maa. Please," I pleaded.

"All this is nothing but a farce. Look how your father is wasting our hard-earned money. Back home, we are struggling to make ends meet. We eat the same food, day after day. I haven't bought a new *saree* for ages. The only *sarees* that I have are given by my sister. I have to budget the money to buy pencils and notebooks for you and Joy. And look what your father is doing here. I can't see this wastage of money. It is too painful for me. Apart from all this non-sense, I also don't want you to miss your school. Enough is enough."

We left the next day without saying a word to anyone. We saw the sun rising from inside the bus. Mum was upset and I wanted to cheer her up.

I leaned against her shoulder and said, "I will do whatever you say and will never complain."

"You better do that. See what all I am going through to bring you both up. You can't let me down. I am alive because of you and Joy. You better use your time and energy in making your life worth living," that was all that Mum said to me while returning from Rengali.

All employees in Rampur colliery were provided houses, called quarters allocated by the Central Government of India. The employees didn't have to pay money for the quarters. We were lucky because even though my father was gone for months, we weren't asked to evict. But deep inside, Mum had a lingering fear that sooner or later, we were going to be asked to move out. She had talked to me about it a couple of times. One Monday morning, Mum made a quick trip to my father's office to tell them about our situation. My father's boss was a gentleman in his late fifties. He was a nice guy, treated Mum like his daughter. He assured us that they would keep my father's job no matter what.

This time, my father didn't stay away that long. His office sent him an important notice addressed to his parents' address. I am not sure if it was a policy in his office to send letters like that or his boss had devised a plan to bring him back. My father had no option but to return home in less than two months. He abandoned the project of writing the book for the saint and came back to save his job.

Strangely, he didn't behave in a rude way for the first few weeks. He wasn't affectionate or overly loving or anything like that. He listened to us and joined us during mealtimes. Over all, it was pleasant. He even started contributing a portion of his salary towards household expenses on a regular basis. I thanked God every day before going to bed.

Chapter Nine

Harbinger of Hopes and Dreams

One afternoon, when I was helping Mum to hang the washed clothes on a thick rope tied between two Guava trees in our backyard, my father came and said, "It will be nice if we get more money."

I looked at Mum and started to wonder if he was going to ask her to get money from her parents. But he didn't.

"I have a decent job, but I need more money. Going forward, I want to contribute to the *ashram* every month," he said.

"Okay," was all that she could murmur. Mum didn't seem very interested.

I was astonished that Mum agreed to it so easily but was also glad that Mum didn't make a big deal of it. With all honesty, the last thing I wanted was a fight between my parents and anything that could remotely disturb our family dynamics.

"I am planning on writing a series of accountancy exams. My office has all the information about it. The deal is that if I clear them, then I would get promotions, and eventually, get better positions and would be able to move up in the hierarchy. Some of these exams are difficult. But I know I have it in me to ace them all. Moreover, there aren't many people in this field who have passed these, so, I have really good prospects," my father said.

Mum encouraged him. So there began a new chapter of our lives. We were not allowed to make any noise in the evenings after that day.

But all said and done, it was a joy to see him motivated and raring to go. I could easily say without a shadow of a doubt that I loved to see my father study. He seemed so engrossed and he loved learning new concepts. He was content and as a result, everything was peaceful at home.

At times, my heart was overwhelmed with happiness as tranquility prevailed in my house. Only I knew how much I had longed for it. I wanted to soak it all in, right to my bones.

School

India has twenty-two official languages and hundreds of other prominent ones. The two most important languages in India are English and Hindi.

My school was an English medium school and second language was Hindi. The smartest kids were well versed in both languages. I was good in English, but I had no help in Hindi. Mum didn't know the language either. I tried learning it as much as I could on my own, but I had a long way to go.

I had a strong feeling that our Hindi teacher in middle school, Mr. Sharma, didn't like me much.

I had convinced myself saying, *Well why should he? I wasn't good in the subject after all! This is how things are going to be during my school year and it will never change!*

With time, I realized that I wasn't the only person he didn't like. There were some more students, too. He had gotten used to nettle us with his harsh comments.

If I wished him, "Good Morning," he looked away in a different direction. If I had a genuine question in the subject, he said, "I am busy doing something. Come back later." I found myself vulnerable at school. But those tough days opened my eyes big and wide as I prepared for life.

I told Mum once, "I am the scapegoat. It's fine. I can never get better in the subject. I am not meant for that."

"Keep trying, Lismun," Mum said lovingly.

I have to admit that there were times when I found Mr. Sharma hilarious, too. He was my father's age. He was tall, with brown eyes, and carried a small comb in his pocket. He didn't hesitate it to ask the students how he looked.

Amidst all this, I was exceling in other subjects, but my confidence was zero about my Hindi homework and assignments. If I wrote a synopsis, I thought my handwriting wasn't good. If I wrote in my best possible handwriting, I thought my interpretation wasn't good. I was very critical about my work. Most of my days were filled with confusions about Hindi grammar such as figuring the gender part of non-living things.

Mum said, "Learning a language is not rocket science. Speak the language, write it, and practice more. You haven't been exposed to the language, and that's why you find it hard. Practice and you can learn as many languages as you want."

I loved the fact that Mum encouraged me, but I got frustrated as I didn't have a tutor.

One night, I was frustrated with Hindi homework and complained to Mum about it, "I really need help, Maa. I can't do this homework by myself. It is too difficult for me."

"I will find a tutor for you."

And she did. His name was Mr. Mishra. He was a retired, middle school, Hindi teacher. He had a group of eleven students, including Pali. He was already teaching some students from my school when I joined the group.

Every evening, we gathered in Ruby's house, a sixth grader from my school. We sat round him in a circle as he screamed at us. Ruby's mother brought coffee and some snacks, mostly cashew sweets thirty minutes into our session. So, the second half of teaching was mostly done with food in his mouth. Pali and I found it hilarious.

But the best part of those tutoring sessions was spending time with Pali. Ruby's house was a seven-minute walk from my home, but Pali and I took more than an hour to go home. We loved gazing at the stars and talking. Those were beautiful moments with my childhood best friend.

A few weeks later when we were waiting for the school bus to come and take us home, I told Pali and Anna how perfect my life had become.

Anna said, "Good for you, girl. I am so happy to hear that."

My Father and Accountancy Exams

While preparing for the exams, my father was in good mood most days. He was busy with his books if he wasn't working in the office. After coming back home, he drank his tea and went straight to his desk to study. Evening dinners were good, too, because he showed genuine interest in my coursework and asked about my grades. It made me happy that he wanted to know about my performance and my life.

One evening while eating dinner, my father said with great pride, "I love Statistics. Analyzing data is fun."

He didn't have a background in math and science, so accounting was a purely a new subject for him. He started everything from scratch. But we were all happy to see him excited about something that was going to help the whole family in the long run. With all honesty, I loved that side of my father, as a go-getter who aced his exams.

He got great scores in the first two written tests. The day his results were announced, he bought sweets for all of us. It was around that time when the fundamentals of statistics were introduced in my math syllabus at school. He taught me mean, media, and mode. It was the first time he taught me something and that, too, with patience. I took great pride in telling other kids that I learned them all from my father.

One night before dinner as I helped Mum set the table, she looked at me with absolute pride and said, "Do you see your father now? He turned around one hundred eighty degrees."

I couldn't be happier.

When I continued getting perfect scores in math, I became my math teacher's favorite student. Strangely, I started looking forward to going to school. I didn't care about what Mr. Sharma thought of me anymore.

As my father passed the initial exams, he needed more space and time at home. Our house was a tiny one-bedroom quarter. With two kids, sometimes it was difficult for him to concentrate. His boss knew about this, so, he decided to do something.

It turned out that one of the employees' homes near Pali's house was vacant. So, they offered it to my father to study during evenings.

Sometimes, Mum sent food for him while he studied, which I carried in a basket. All I had to do was to cross a street, hop over a wall, and I was there. Delivering food to my father had its own perks. I got to play with my friend, Pali, who lived in the adjacent home.

The house where my father studied was pretty much empty. It had a table, a chair, and a refrigerator. It got cold during wintertime though. Mum was an expert in stitching clothes and sweaters. So, she made a couple of thick, red, woolen sweaters for him. Some nights, when it was super cold, Mum asked me to take blankets for him, and I did it.

Those were blissful days. I loved the stability and calmness in my house. It was like we were all working together towards a dream, our dream!

Summer 1988

It was a Friday afternoon. The school playground echoed with the giggles and laughter of children. Some kids ran around the playground playing tag, some kids sat down under the big, *Banyan* tree in the shade and talked, and some kids played basketball.

"My only goal this summer is to sleep," Pali announced.

"Well, I want to finish up some books. I have a list ready," I said.

"I am done reading kids' books. I want to get some romantic novels from the library or the book store."

We giggled.

"Let's play." Anna said.

"Basketball?" Pali asked.

"Alright!" I said little loudly with excitement.

We were a bunch of girls playing happily when Pali and I got distracted because we saw an ice-cream vendor outside the school campus. That's when I was knocked out by another player.

At that moment, I didn't realize it was an accident and I thought it was intentional. I don't know how I mustered the courage, but I got up, dusted my skirt, and pushed the girl with all my strength to the ground in retaliation. I couldn't believe I did it. I had always been a fragile child physically. Did I really push her? The rush of confidence I felt was something that could never be explained in words.

She screamed and cried as if I had broken every bone in her body. Right that moment, I knew I was in trouble.

That evening, I told my parents about what happened in school.

"But she pushed me first."

"Did she do it intentionally?" Mum asked.

"I am not sure, Maa. I didn't like her pushing me on the ground and I pushed her back. Maybe I was standing up for myself."

"Why do you think so, Lismun?"

"I know she did it intentionally because she never apologized to me."

Next day, my teacher sent a message that they wanted to talk to my parents.

"I will talk to your teacher," my father said while chewing a piece of fried fish and looking at the television.

I had a slightest hope that my father would side with me because after all, I was his daughter. I thought in the worst case he would get angry for some time. I didn't know what was the outcome of that meeting going be.

When my father talked to the teacher, the result was what I had feared the most; My teacher said I shouldn't have pushed her back. When my father came back home, he blamed me and shouted at me.

"I did it in retaliation. I swear by God, I didn't start the fight. I swear, Papa," I said that countless times. I cried and pleaded but my words fell on his deaf ears.

But he wasn't willing to hear anything that night.

I wasn't sure what triggered my father's anger, the fact that I was blamed or I argued back with him. He took some old newspaper from the side table and hit my face so hard that my hair flew up and Joy started laughing.

"She looks funny. Her hair is standing up," he said.

It was far from being funny. I had a hard time digesting that fact that my father refused to believe my side of the story. That incident wounded me deeply. What happened that moment was something that remained in my mind forever, like a thorn pricking me every once in a while.

I found Mum watching me from the kitchen. She blew me a kiss and I knew that my eyes and sad voice affected her. But she put a finger on her lips. That angered me. She didn't stand up for me. I felt alone and extremely sad. I was up for a long time that night. I didn't have a diary, but I wrote on my notebook. I poured my heart. I was actually angry! Parents are supposed to take care of their kids not hurt them. Period. I was only eleven.

Next day, Mum and I had some quiet time together while drinking tea. "I can't believe that you didn't stand up for me last night," I said.

"Lisa, you and I both know how catastrophic it can be when we go against your father's commands."

"What did you see in him? Why did you marry him, Maa? He believes the whole world but not his wife and kids. Sometimes, I hate him so much."

"I didn't see any of that in him when I got married. I was so young. Let's give our best and make the most of today. Finish your tea and go to school. Keep your emotions separate from the job you have at hand. I know it's hard, but it is doable."

I paused for a bit and asked Mum, "Forget about Papa. How do I deal with a teacher who does not like me?"

"Why do you think he dislikes you?" Mum asked me.

"See, that's the point, I don't understand. I have always been very respectful to him."

"Then think hard about why he dislikes you."

"I am sorry, Mum. I can't find any reason."

"Think carefully."

"I can't find any. Why are you forcing me to give explanations when there isn't one?"

"See, that's the thing. You are going to have people like him all your life who will dislike you without any apparent reason. There will be people who will love you and bring out the best in you, and then there will be people who will leave no stone unturned to bring out the worst in you. It depends on you how you react to them."

"Have you come across people like that?"

I paused.

"I mean, Maa, let's exclude Papa from this topic," I asked her again.

Mum smiled, "Yes, let's take your father out of this discussion. Of course, I meet people like that all the time. People who want to see me sad, people who don't like me without any reason or rhyme. It's okay. It happens. They have brains, and they are free to process any type of thought they want."

"I don't know why some people are just mean."

"To tell you the truth, I don't know either. If I knew, I would have fixed your father by now."

Then we burst into peals of laughter. Sometimes, I just loved how funny Mum was. It always lightened up the burden of pathos I carried in my aching heart.

A new realization dawned on me when I went to school that morning. I was glad I could speak to Mum about what I felt deep in my heart. If I felt that Mum didn't understand what I felt, I always had my notebook to write about my biggest fears and darkest secrets. I am thankful that I was forced to learn those lessons early on in life.

Miraculously, the throbbing headache didn't bother me much. I managed to smile when I entered inside the classroom that morning.

For the next couple of months, my father worked nearly eighteen hours a day. He had office during daytime and his evenings were busy with books. We hardly saw him at home. And his moods were highly unpredictable when was with us. There were days when he was happy as he was working towards a goal and then there were days when he lost patience, even when we made the slightest noise.

Mum told him, "Take it slow. You need your sleep."

He always had an answer ready, "Nope, I want all the three promotions. I have to slog and here is no way out."

One evening, when I asked for two new notebooks, he snapped, "Why do you need new notebooks? Do you think money grows on the trees? If you run out of notebooks, write on the floor with chalk."

Like most days, Mum came to my rescue and said, "Tell me what you need. I will get it for you. Your father is working too hard. Don't go to him for anything."

Mum bought me four notebooks while coming back from work the next day. I never complained or asked for anything from my father after that.

Something Clicked!

I spent the happiest days with Pali. We ran on the open fields in front of her house. We ate corn dogs, made sandcastles, and sang songs during our free time. Pali was a good singer, and her family had a pretty good collection old Bollywood movie songs. We spent many summer evenings singing songs on her front lawn. Her mother was an expert in making egg noodles and potato fries. As my father was busy with his exams and Mum was busy with Joy, I spent a good chunk of my evenings at her place. Those memories of leisure evenings were some of the best in my childhood.

School was almost over, and I was done with sixth grade. We had one more week until summer holidays. Mum was planning on taking us to my grandparents' house during summer vacation. I enjoyed spending my summer holidays in Grandpa's house, eating mangoes, playing on the terrace with my cousin sister, and drinking *chai*.

It was during the last week of school. I was playing with Pali and Anna under the scorching sun. I realized I needed to fill up my water bottle. As I ran towards the water fountain inside the building, I tripped and fell because of my untied shoelace.

I sat down to tie it, and suddenly, I saw someone's big brown shoes in front of me. I lifted my head up and there he was, Mr. Sharma!

I wondered what he had in his mind when he raised his eyebrows and said in the most mocking voice, "Why do you keep falling all the time? Maybe some people are meant to fall."

His sadistic face was the most awful thing I had ever seen. At that moment, something strange happened, something clicked, and something inside me changed. As if I saw an electric switch and everything was lit up around me. The world around me froze, and the earth came to a standstill.

I had done absolutely nothing to him. I was an obedient student, I was sincere, and showed him the utmost respect. But more than anything else, I tried hard to do well in his subject. I took notes in the class. And there he was, right in front of me, with a grin on his face, waiting for me to cry.

As I stared at him that day, it was crystal clear that he wanted to see my reaction. He expected me to be puzzled, angry, and sad. I was determined that I was not going to give him that feeling of victory come what may.

I looked into his eyes, I didn't cry, I didn't speak a word, just looked at him. I don't know if it made him uncomfortable, but he waited to see for a few more minutes if I had tears in my eyes. When I didn't sob, he left.

I sat on the playground long after he was gone. It was a very hot day, but somehow, that didn't bother me. I promised myself that someday I was going to excel in Hindi. I had to prove it to myself. It was a promise I was going to live up to, no matter what.

At home, Mum made it easier for me. She said, "Don't take things personally. The way people treat you tells a lot about themselves. It has nothing to do with you. Just ignore him."

I was blessed to have a mother I could share my problems with. After that day, it really didn't bother me much what Mr. Sharma said and what he did. To me, he really didn't exist. I became good at ignoring his nasty comments. When he laughed at me, I looked out of the window. And then, he felt offended.

He said, "Look here, look at me. Why are you looking out of the window?"

I looked at him, listened to what he was saying, and then looked out of the window again. It continued for a couple of weeks. It was strange, but in two weeks or so, he stopped picking on me, except for some snide remarks here and there.

Chapter Ten

Books on Fire

One week later, on the last day of the school year, I found Mum crying in the kitchen corner when I arrived home. Joy looked sad, too. I couldn't figure out what had happened but my father was livid with rage, back to his old self. He was looking for something,

"Can I help you find something, Papa?"

"Yes, I want a matchbox," he said.

"For what?"

"Oh, nothing! I want to start the stove. Get the matchbox ready. I need to get something from inside the house."

"Okay. I know where Mum keeps them."

As I gave him the match box, Mum came out from behind the door of the living room and held my hand tight.

"He is insane. Nobody can save him."

"Why Maa?" I whispered.

"Because he is just insane, he is mad and crazy," Mum said with anger in her voice.

I could hardly understand what Mum said. I just hugged her and cried. My father didn't hear what my mum said as he was inside. As I tried to process the gravity of the situation, I saw my father gathering all his books on the desk in a bedsheet. Within seconds, he ran towards the backyard, threw the big pile of books on the ground and set his books and notes on fire.

All I could say was, "Please, Papa. Please, stop. Please, stop."

He looked at me angrily and said, "Your Mum made the worst lunch today. I stayed home to finish up few chapters and she couldn't even make some good food for me? It is ridiculous! I am not writing these exams anymore. I am done with all this non-sense."

He kept talking gibberish as I jumped around, trying to save some of his notes and books while burning my fingers. Mum did nothing, she neither stopped me nor talked to my father. She sat there in silence, with tears streaming down her cheeks. Joy sat on her lap and stared at her face.

I ran to the bathroom and got as many buckets of water as I could to extinguish the fire, but I could hardly save a couple of books.

That night my father said, "I am done with these exams. So glad I destroyed the books."

My head spun in all directions as I heard his painful words. The fire was gone with water, but the flame rose high in the sky and everything flew away in that black smoke. Everything, our dreams, our hopes, and even the flicker of promise that life had shown towards us.

Mum and I slept together that night and I held her tight. She said without batting an eyelash, "This is what anger does to human beings. All this because he didn't get his favorite food?"

"But why didn't you say you were sorry to him? Why didn't you try to save those books? Why, Maa? I think you are responsible, too," I was confused that Mum didn't do anything to stop the fire.

"No, Lismun. I am tired of his madness. His anger is his problem, not mine."

"I feel scared at times, like anything can change. Life sucks," I said.

"Yes, life sucks. That's why you need to focus on your own life. Don't worry what changes or does not change around you. You need to build your own life in a way that you can't wake up to live it," Mum said with a stoic face.

I had nothing to say after that. I was extremely sad that night. All my hopes were crushed and there was nothing to look forward to. As I wrote on my notebook that night, I had tears dripping from my eyes and kept messing up my handwriting. When I got tired, I went to bed. I cried so much that my eyes ached, and my heart bled.

A few days later, my father made a trip to his parents' home. When he came back, he said, "I love my parents. They support my decision to write the book on the saint."

After my father's visit to his parents' house, there was no looking back for him. He sent all his money to the saint and to his parents.

One evening, he went on a rampage breaking things, because he didn't like how the house looked. He threw plates, clothes, food, anything and everything he could get his hands on. He threw them at us, he threw them at the walls, and everywhere. He did it for nearly thirty minutes, without paying heed to what was hitting whom. Once he was tired, he left the house.

We were too tired to find where he spent the night or maybe we didn't care.

Mum said, "We all need a break from each other. Let things cool down a bit. It's okay if he spends the night far from us."

We held each other tight on the bed but found it hard to fall asleep. Mum put on some music and we danced. All three of us. Strangely, it felt good, real good. Mum wasn't a student of psychology, but she always came up with these amazing ways to overcome our deepest pain.

Once we had exhausted our energy, we didn't remember how we fell asleep. Next day, when we got up, it was a regular day as if nothing had happened. We went to school. My father was back home in the evening, like any regular day. Nobody asked any questions. Nobody talked. We ate dinner in silence. It felt good though. Silence was gold.

And life went on, days flew, months passed, and Joy and I grew up little taller. A little stronger mentally and physically! Mum was busy in bringing us up single-handedly.

Mum became a cornucopia of love, strength and courage. She wore hopes in her eyes and carried dreams in her heart. Mum couldn't afford to buy anything for us as she was saving a chunk of her salary for our higher education.

The only thing she bought from the grocery store was rice and milk. She learned to prepare vegetable curry by cooking weeds from the garden. We drank tea without sugar and we ate food without salt. When we were hungry, we ate plain rice with homemade pickles. We didn't starve but those were tough days, but we were tougher. We survived. All my whining and tantrums stopped when I saw Mum standing tall and refusing to give up.

Fall and Winter 1988

After my father burnt his books, he went back to being his old self. All his niceness was gone. When the evil came out, it came out stronger. More bitter and vicious!

But one good thing happened, because my father had cleared two exams, he got a major promotion and we moved into a two-bedroom house. It was quite spacious, and I had my own room. I was happy because having my own room meant seeing my father less.

When I turned eleven in July that year, he didn't even wish me a happy birthday.

Mum said, "It's okay. Don't worry about your father not wishing you happy birthday."

It might have been easy for her to say but it was hard for me to experience. I couldn't comprehend why he couldn't say a few good words to me on my birthday; after all, he was one of the two people who created me.

Truth was that I often blamed myself when I didn't get the love I truly deserved. I spent a lot of time wondering if I did something wrong or what I could do differently. The thing is that there wasn't anything that made my father happy because he didn't care for us.

I didn't skip school. Mum made some sugar cookies for me and I took them for my classmates.

One of the girls who lived near my house smiled and said, "These cookies look great. Let's celebrate Lisa's birthday."

So, that's how I distributed cookies that morning.

When I came home, Mum asked, "Did your friends like the cookies?"

"Yes, Mum. They did."

A week before Christmas that year, I received a letter from Grandpa. When my teacher gave me the letter, a light gleamed on my face. Grandpa wrote that he would come to pick me up during Christmas vacation and that made my day. I was so exuberant that I started to cry in the middle of the class because he had sent the letter to me, to my school address. It was the first time when someone had written a letter to me and that meant the world to me. When I came back home that day, I ran inside the house to show the letter to Mum. She returned my gesture with a hug.

"Sure, my dear. You will have a great time with your grandparents. You need a break from school and from this house, too. You really do," Mum said delightedly.

Mum had assumed that my father was outside the house, but he was in the bedroom. He heard everything that we talked about. He came out of the room and he looked like a statue of wrath, a volcano about to erupt.

He snatched the letter from me and read it one more time loudly. We knew well that he liked to control everything around him, and as he read line after line, I started to get more and more frightened. I thought I was going to have a panic attack. I started to cry.

He went back to the bedroom, lugged the two big suitcases from under the bed and started packing them with his clothes. I was bawling my eyes out and freaking out.

"I am leaving this house now. I will rent a place and live on my own," he screamed.

I begged him not to leave the house.

"It's just a letter. Look, Lisa, will not go if you don't want her to. Don't make a big deal out of it," Mum tried to be logical with him.

"Lisa, you always wanted to know why I don't like you, right? Well, here is the reason. I don't like you because you support your mum for everything. And I don't like your mum because she is her father's daughter. I hate that man with every fiber in my body. He should be paying for his daughter and his grandkids, but he never sends any money."

"I am sorry, Papa, I really am. I will not go anywhere. I promise you that," I was almost stammering.

But Mum didn't say anything after that. She just looked out of the window. It was obvious that she didn't like what my father said about Grandpa. She remained quiet; my father hauled his luggage in a cab. Her face reflected defeat, waves of shock, total disbelief, helplessness, and pain.

"I have to get out of this house. I am writing a book and I need to be alone," my father said.

"Papa, will you come back after your book is done?" I was shivering by now.

"No," he said and was out of the house.

In just ten minutes or so, my father was gone. His shadow had disappeared. All this happened within thirty minutes. Mum stood there with both her hands on us, looking at the front door that had sprung open with my father's departure. I was appalled and completely shaken that a small letter could create such havoc.

Joy had been playing in the living room, dressed only in underpants. That angry avatar of my father scared him so much that he urinated, and it dripped from his underwear.

Mum looked at us calmly and said, "Time for bed, kids." All three of us slept on the same bed that night. As I laid there awake, I thought how distorted life was becoming. I thought about my father and how easily he was swayed by anger. Mum sat on the bedside for a long time that night.

I felt responsible for my father leaving us. But Mum said, "You have nothing to do with it, Lismun. He just wanted an excuse to leave. Don't worry about it."

But school was tough. Kids talked about my father. Sometimes, they asked me straight to my face, "Is your father staying in a different house?" I wasn't well equipped to deal with it. The only way I could react was to pretend that I didn't hear anything and just looked away.

But then, there were few kids who were really caring, including Pali and Anna. They never asked me anything about my father, neither in private nor in public. I was eternally grateful to them and carried an unuttered 'Thank you' in my heart for them.

When Pali got some Bundi laddoo, she saved a portion of it for me, knowing every well how much I loved it. Those little things kept me going.

Chapter Eleven

November 1989, Joy in the Residential school

It had been close to four months since my father left. We came to know from a family friend that he had rented a small flat, not far from where we lived. His office was right behind our house. I saw him coming out of his office building many evenings when I played outside, but he never waved at me. When Mum counted every penny, he withdrew his complete salary on the last day of the month and walked past the house without bothering even a wink how his family survived. While we were grasping at straws, my father didn't bother even once to know if we needed anything. He kept no contact.

One night, while tucking us in bed, Mum leaned over my head and said, "Take care of your health. Don't eat food straight from the fridge. Don't get drenched in rain. I have no money for hospital visits if you get asthma attacks."

I nodded, and she kissed my forehead. Her tear drops fell all on my cheeks. I was figuring out the right words to say when Mum said, "I am struggling financially. I will not be able to make it without your help."

To me, it felt like a huge responsibility. I kept quiet and looked at Mum's shadow that was cast on the wall until I fell asleep with a wet feeling on my cheeks while Mum sat there.

Some of my father's colleagues lived in the neighborhood. I sent a few letters and notes to him through them. Unfortunately, I never got any reply. A friend of his told us that he spent most of his time worshipping God and spent his free time writing his book.

The proverb '*He was so heavenly minded that he was no earthly good*' was apt for him.

In midst of all this, Joy and I were doing well in school. I was thriving in all subjects except Hindi. Mum's way of encouraging us was to call both us "Rising stars."

I had an old math book for course that Mum had got from one of her friends. It was falling apart and didn't have some pages of trigonometry. One evening, after coming back from school, I opened the book and it didn't have the pages I wanted to study for a test the next day. Knowing very well how tight we were on the monetary front, I decided to borrow it from a classmate.

I walked almost a mile in my torn slippers to get the book. My classmate didn't let me come inside her house because my feet were dirty. She told me that her mother would be angry if my dusty and muddy feet made her floor unclean. I smiled, thanked her, and came back home.

I didn't mention about the incident or my torn slippers to Mum. I told her about it only when my test result came out, a perfect score.

Mum said, "Good job, Lismun. Go and give her the book back. Or leave it on the front porch."

It was the first time I saw Mum sob after seeing my math score.

I said, "Okay."

"Nobody respects poor people," Mum murmured.

Deep inside, Mum and I knew well that the ground below our feet was swampy. An uncertain future was something that troubled us the most. Mum looked lost as if she was in a different world. I would be talking to her about something, and she would just drift away.

One afternoon, she took a lot of unnecessary furniture and sold it. She was calm most of the times but got mad if we wasted food.

"Finish every grain of food on your plate. I earn money with my sweat and blood. I can't see it wasted. You better listen to me and if you don't, then the consequences will be bad, pretty bad!" was her standard statement.

I don't think the real problem was her low salary. The problem was that a lot of elementary school teachers employed by the state government weren't paid regularly. Some days, I felt that there was no shore within our sight. Some days, I felt the shore was shrouded in mist. But in spite of all those uncertainties, I thought that it was wonderful not to walk on eggshells constantly and be afraid of my father's wrath.

Every evening, she sat down with us while we finished our homework. She loved knitting and I loved stretching out my legs in a way that it touched her legs, too, while Joy leaned on her back. Moments like those were priceless.

Three people tied together with an unbreakable bond that was all surpassing, all conquering, and all powerful. Little did we know that it was short lived.

It was Monday. I woke up to the beautiful blaze of sunlight falling on my face. I loved that feeling. Maybe that's why I always left the curtain on my windows open in the night. The gleams of sunlight gave me strength and I started my day promising myself that I was going to give my best and push myself further in school.

When I entered inside the classroom that morning, my science teacher asked me to go to the principal's room. I was so nervous that I skipped a heartbeat.

My school principal was a former math teacher and was an amazing human being. He had seen me working on my school assignments while other kids played outside during recess, so he wanted to find out why I never played outside.

"Have a seat, Lisa."

"Thank you, sir."

"Why don't you play outside during recess?"

"I don't know, sir. I can't play. I meant I can't run too much. I get tired easily."

I tried to push my fear into the back of my head and answered it with honesty.

"Why not?" he asked with his raised eyebrows.

"The problem is that..." I murmured.

"Yes, go on. I am listening. What is the problem?"

"The problem is that I don't like running. I just like being in the classroom. I like my quiet time."

"But playing outside is good for you."

"Sometimes when it rains outside, kids get drenched. I don't want to get wet."

"Why not? Rain is fun, too. Don't you think so? You should have all types of experiences in life."

"Because..."

"Because, what, my child?"

"We are in a tight financial situation now. Mum can't take me to the hospital if I get sick," I had eased a little bit by then and answered his questions with confidence.

"I want you to play outside. Every day. If it rains, come inside. If you get drenched and get a cold, I will take you to the doctor."

It was the first time I saw a teacher in my school with tears in his eyes because my words touched him.

"You know, I used to be a math teacher?" he said, changing the topic.

"Yes, sir. I know."

"I hear that you ace your math tests. I am proud of you."

"Thank you, sir," I said, wiping my tears.

"You can always come and talk to me whenever you feel like it. But do go out and play. Fresh air is good. You don't have to run if you don't like. I want you to know that I know about your family situation. I think you are doing a fabulous job. Your mother must be proud of you."

I was relieved and happy to hear that. I nodded with great pride as I walked out of his office. I could hardly hide my big smile. But the smile disappeared as quickly as it had come. I saw my father standing in front of the office.

"Hi Papa. Nice to see you," I greeted him while coming out.

"I am here to see your principal," he said in a voice that made it clear that he didn't want to talk to me.

"Papa, will you come home tonight?"

"First of all, tell me something. Why were you in the principal's office? Did you do something wrong?"

"You know he really likes me. He just told me that."

"I don't care what he thinks about you," his voice grew louder.

"I am sorry, Papa. I answered it because you asked me a question. I didn't want to upset you," I said.

Such words from my father weren't new to me, and I wasn't a bit surprised. I kept my cool.

"Okay, let me go and talk to Joy now,"

"What do you have to talk about?" I asked him because I was sensing something fishy.

"I am taking Joy to my place," My father declared.

"What?" I asked. I panicked.

"I am taking him for two days. I want to spend time with him, just play with him, take him for ice-cream. It will be fun. Just father and son."

I was so naive and selfless. I became so happy that I couldn't believe what I was hearing.

"Really? That's wonderful. Joy will be so happy. I will take you to his classroom. Come this way," I was delighted beyond words.

Even before I could finish my sentence, my father shrugged me off.

He said, "I can find Joy's classroom. You don't have to show it to me. I need to sign the permission papers and do all the formalities. Go back to your classroom. I can't talk to you right now."

"Okay, Papa. I can run home and get some of Joy's clothes. Do you want me to do that?" I said it with an intent to help.

"No need to bring his clothes. I will buy some new ones for Joy."

I was still happy and it did not bother me a bit that my father was excluding me. I was just happy that my brother was going to have a nice time with him, something I could never have. I was totally okay with it. So that afternoon, my father took Joy straight from school. I assumed that he was going to buy him clothes.

That evening I went home alone. Mum was near the gate, watering the plants. Usually, I carried two school backpacks, mine and Joy's while Joy came behind me, jumping and kicking his ball. But that evening I had only one backpack.

"Where is Joy?" Mum was so nervous that she could barely talk.

I ran and hugged her.

"Mum, you will not believe it. Papa was in the school today. He came to take Joy to spend a couple of days with him. I mean just to do fun stuff, to visit a few places, have ice-cream and all that."

"What? He never told me about it. Joy is so little. He is only five. He has never lived without me," she said fighting back her tears.

"Relax, Maa. Let's be happy for Joy. He is with Papa and he deserves it. They are going to have a great time together. Can you fix me a quick meal? I am really starving. Rice is fine," I assured her.

As Mum fixed my meal, she watched me from the corner of her eye. I was genuinely happy for Joy and was wondering what they would be doing that evening as I sharpened my pencils and waited for food.

"I feel a strange lump of fear stuck in my throat," Mum said as she cooked.

"It will be okay, Mum. We both know that he loves Joy."

"Maybe I am thinking too much. Maybe it is not a big deal. Maybe they are really having a nice time," Mum sounded more like she was talking to herself and reassuring herself.

Joy didn't come back the next day or the day after that. When he didn't come for four days, Mum called my father. We found out that his landline phone was disconnected. After waiting for one week, Mum went straight to his office to meet him, but he was not in the office. He was on leave.

When Mum inquired more, she discovered he hadn't come to work for one week. By now, she was at her wit's end. She had a hard time believing that he could be so vengeful that he felt the need to take it out on a five-year-old little boy.

We knew that the kidnapping was done to alienate Joy and Mum and to control her indirectly. At that point, Mum was willing to do anything to get Joy. The only problem was that she could not reach out to my father. She didn't have a single ounce of information about his whereabouts.

Mum was scared that the trauma inflicted on Joy was going to scar him for life. Finally, after two weeks, we got a call from my father's Mom. She explained what had happened. That Monday, after picking up Joy from school, my father took him straight to his parents' house in Sonepur. After staying there for a few days, my father got Joy admitted in a residential school one hundred miles from where we lived. She told us the name of the school but refused to give more details. When Mum asked about my father and his intentions, my father's mother hung up on Mum.

That weekend, Mum spent every single waking hour, calling people and asking them if they knew anything about my father. Unfortunately, nobody knew. Mum went to all his colleagues' houses to get more information and I accompanied her. As much as I missed my little brother, I wanted Mum to be at peace. Those were tough days, and I carried a pool of tears inside me. One moment, there was an urge to cry; next moment, I was strong and determined to fight back. I prayed to God for a miracle where all our problems just disappeared.

Mum had stopped eating, even though she cooked for me. She looked frighteningly thin. That became the scariest reality of my entangled life. There was a depth of pain that I carried below my skin. It was ready to erupt anytime. Some days, I was everything to Mum. Some days I was a nobody, as if I didn't exist.

It was time for mid-year exams. As I had spent the whole weekend going around with Mum to get some information about my father, I decided to stay up late that night and study. It was around midnight when I heard some strange noises coming from Mum's bedroom. Scared, I pushed the door little bit. The lights were on and I saw Mum sitting on the floor, her hair totally unkempt, wailing while holding the pillows tight, as if she was howling in pain. She was so lost that she didn't even realize that I was near the door. I rushed inside the bedroom to comfort her. But she was lost and all she could say was, "I want Joy back! I want my son back!" and it didn't matter how tightly I held her or what I told her.

"Mum, why don't you report it to the police?" I asked her bluntly.

Mum wiped her tears, "I can't. I am afraid your father would harm Joy. He is capable of anything."

"Why do you think he took Joy, Maa?"

"Because he wanted to torture me. All this while, I felt he loved Joy. But he does not. If he really loved Joy, he would have kept Joy with him. But look at him, he sent Joy to a residential school. Can you imagine a little kid in a residential school?"

I had not thought of the severity of the problem. There was a slight glimmer of hope that someday Joy would be back, but now she did not have any attachment to the world.

The impulse to run out of the door and use our neighbor's phone to call Grandpa struck me. But it was midnight. I don't remember when I fell asleep. Next morning, when I woke up, I was on the floor. I found Mum packing a small carry-on bag.

"Mum, are we going somewhere? I have an exam today," I asked her in a very irritating voice.

"I know you have an exam. You will stay at the neighbor's house tonight. I am going to Joy's school and from there, I will go to your father's parents' house. I am sure they know something about his whereabouts. I need to figure out what he is doing and why he put Joy in the residential school."

My neighbor's daughter, Rimi, was my classmate. I liked Rimi and I think Rimi liked me, too. I stayed in their house when Mum was gone. I understood why Mum had to leave me back, but I felt lonely and anxious. I prayed to God that she came back with some good news.

Mum was back a couple of days later. I was dying to hear some good news about Joy.

"Mum, do you have any news?"

"Yes, I do," she replied.

"What's the news?"

There was no answer. She left her blue bag on the living room floor and headed straight to the bathroom. She took out a pile of clothes from the corner and started washing them.

"Mum, what's wrong with you? Why are you doing this now? It is ten in the night. You just came from Sonepur now. Let's go to sleep."

"No, I need to wash these right now."

"Why Mum? Why now?" I got irritated by her eccentric behavior.

"Because I can't focus. I can't sleep. I can't do anything else. Let me finish up the chores," she screamed at me and pushed me away. I knew Mum didn't mean it. She was frustrated and she took it out on me.

"Maa, what has happened to you? I know you are very sad and you miss Joy. But I am here. You act as if my life does not matter."

"Nothing matters now. I miss Joy," Mum closed the water tap and left the half-washed clothes on the floor as they were.

"I want to go and see Joy. But I can't."

"Why not?"

"Because I am scared of your father. He has told the school principal that Joy's mother is dead and there is nobody to take care of him."

"What? And the school principal believed it? He must be a stupid guy."

"It really doesn't matter what he thinks. He believed your father. I spoke to him on the phone. He thought I was a fake person."

"Wait a minute. You got the school principal's number? How?"

"It's not that difficult. You can find their phone number from the school directory."

"Mum, you can't let these people win."

"I have already lost this battle."

"You have to be stronger than this. All this while you were my rock. Buckle up, Maa. Let's fight back. If nothing works, think about Joy. Don't you think he is missing you? Why are you so scared in the first place?"

"I am scared because I am afraid your father will do more harm to Joy. What if he takes him so far away from us that we will never see him? What if he takes Joy out of the state or out of the country? There is a lot of stuff you have to learn about life."

That night Mum was so upset that she shut the bedroom door on my face and went to sleep.

I was upset, too. We were both struggling to find our inner strength to cope with the situation. We were both sleep deprived, so the next day I missed school. Mum came back from school early in the afternoon too. She had a throbbing headache. After a few hours of sleep, both of us felt better.

We called Joy's school in the evening after waking up. One of the teachers picked up the phone. She didn't let Mum talk to Joy because he was admitted to the school by my father. She also refused to believe that Mum was genuinely Joy's mother. As if Joy's absence didn't do enough damage, that phone call broke all the strength Mum possessed, and she just went into a shell.

That week, when we were asked to write something on our favorite topic/subject, I wrote a poem about my brother,

'In the flight of my thoughts, I reach out for his tiny hands.
I hold his delicate fingers tight and strong as we cross the road.
In the stairs of my imaginations, we climb the tall mountains, undaunted.
His cute chubby face and sweet voice give me tenacity and make me smile.
In the ocean of life, I stand by his side as he learns to swim.
I give my brother my unconditional love as he searches for the pearls,
But dreams are dreams after all, once my eyes open, I see them shattered in front of me, battered and beaten.
They look like branches fallen from the trees, stomped and stepped on.
As I muster my courage to face the world without my brother, the brutalities of life beat me down, grab me with their tentacles, drain the energy from every fiber of my being.
And train me for another flight of thoughts, another staircase, and another ocean of life.'

Some of my friends in school asked me about Joy. His teachers asked me if he was coming back. I had no answer and that's why I preferred to be quiet.

But deep inside, the silence scared me, and I didn't like it. I felt a constant hammering noise in my head, as if the walls around me were crashing, as if there were demons dancing in front of my eyes. I wanted to run, but there was no escape.

Mum cried constantly. Separating Joy from her was the biggest blow for her. The hurt was thousands fold more because my father committed the heinous crime.

School became my rescue because I drowned myself in books. It was a temporary relief. I liked being busy as long as nobody asked me about Joy. Talking about Joy meant opening up the flood gates.

Home was an altogether different story. Unlike me, Mum hated going outside. She didn't like dragging herself out of the bed to go to work. Mum often told me her feelings overwhelmed her and she had lost the light of her life. It did not matter how beautiful the flowers outside looked or if there were good programs on T.V.

It did not matter how well I had done in my tests. My achievements didn't matter. A vital part of her was dead, and there was nothing I could to revive it. I showered her with hugs and did what I could, but still she sobbed and nothing made her happy.

Mum's behavior destroyed my ebullient self. I understood her immense grief, but I couldn't fathom why she neglected me. It made me very sad. I tried talking to her many times. Some days, she just listened to me with a blank face, and some days, she promised to change. But nothing happened. Things remained like that for a month.

One day, she took all of Joy's clothes, washed them, dried them, and ironed them very neatly. Next day, she put them all back in the closet.

"What's going on, Maa? Why did you wash Joy's clothes and why did you put them back in the closet?" I asked her with utter curiosity.

"Because I miss him, but I also know that he is not here. I have no idea when will he be back," Mum started to sob.

I missed Joy the most when I saw his classmates in school. I wrote letters to him every day and put them in my school postal mail box. Sometimes, the postman in my school offered to put stamps on my letters. But I never received any letter from Joy or his school.

That was a long month. I was tired of being exhausted and I was sick of being feeling stuck.

On a Thursday night, I told Mum, "Let's go and get Joy back, Maa."

"I am not sure about that. I don't think we can bring him," Mum said with a sullen face.

"Maa, you are my rock. Don't break down. Let's go."

Mum didn't say anything, but her face lit up as if that's what she wanted to hear. She agreed and I was pleasantly surprised. That night, we hugged each other and smiled. I knew we were a team forever. We cooked a good dinner for ourselves for the first time in a long time.

"Yes, Lismun. Let's go see him. I am his mum, after all."

"That's the thing! That's exactly what I am saying. You are the most important person in Joy's life. Why are you so timid, Maa? Let's go and get him."

Deep inside, I was glad Mum had me at that point of time. She couldn't have handled it all by herself. I knew it was my turn to be strong. I did my best to support her in any way I could.

Once my school was over on Friday, we took a bus to Joy's residential school. We met another couple in the bus from a nearby village. They were going to bring their daughter home for the weekend. They told us that most of the kids in the school were kids from villages where they didn't have good schools. The definition of a good school those days were "English Medium School," where the primary language taught was English.

When we reached Joy's school, it was dinner time and all kids were lined up with the plates to get dinner. Their faces reflected many different emotions. One little boy was excited as the server filled his plate. A sweet, looking boy near him stared at the floor. Joy was the last kid in the line. He looked the saddest. He had lost weight. He looked like he was sleep deprived and hadn't eaten for days.

The moment Mum saw Joy, she ran to hug him, but one of the teachers stopped her.

"Please wait. You can't meet him," she said sternly.

"But I am his mother," Mum was mad.

"What?"

"I am Joy's mother. I am here to take him."

By now, Joy was crying frantically. They allowed me to go see him because I was a kid. I sat by his side. Ms. Das, one of the teachers who served dinner to the kids, came forward, and took Mum with her.

"Please come with me. You can meet your son and have dinner with him. I can clearly see that you are his mother and you want to go to him. He, too, is dying to hold you tight. We are all human beings. Please come with me."

At that moment, time froze, and I truly believed that there was someone up there looking after Mum, a supernatural power, something stronger, and mightier than life, maybe God!

Ms. Das took all three of us to the common dining hall. Joy sat on Mum's lap and ate his food. I can't remember a single teacher who didn't cry that night.

The school principal, Mr. Tijori, came before bedtime to make sure everything was okay and make rounds and that night wasn't an exception.

Words were just falling on Mum's deaf ears. She didn't care what my father had told Mr. Tijori, nor what he had written in the school admission letter.

"Can I at least take him with me for one night?"

"I am afraid you can't, ma'am!"

My blood boiled. I wanted to pull out his hair out, but he was already bald. Joy held Mum tight and cried for a long time. But we had to leave. Mum kissed him on his forehead and wiped his tears. I hugged him tight and told him to take care of himself. Eventually, Joy wasn't allowed to be with us for that night, and we left without him.

After walking few steps out of the gate, I turned back to see one last glimpse of him. The lights in his room were still on and the moment; he saw my face, he started screaming and crying. We walked away and could hear his gut-wrenching screams for a long time.

That walk was the toughest one of my life. Our minds were blank and spirits were broken and there was nothing to look forward to in life. Mum cried like she had never cried before.

As we boarded the bus that night, I held Mum's hand.

She said, "I feel so broken and there is nothing to look forward to. I left a big chunk of my heart in Joy's school."

"You will always have me, Maa," I said while holding her hand little tighter.

"I will not be able to live without Joy. I miss my baby."

That night we couldn't find seats on the bus, so we stood for almost half the way. A young man offered his seat to me. I wiped my tears and thanked him. I let Mum sit. I stood by her side, still holding her hand tightly, and I could feel the drops of sweat between our palms, yet I didn't let go of the grip.

"Lismun, I have these strange feelings that I had never felt before. I feel someone has poisoned me and I am dying a slow death," Mum said with a face devoid of emotion.

"You need to inform the police, Maa."

One of my mum's distant uncles was a lawyer. Mum met him first thing in the morning, and I accompanied her. She asked about pressing charges against my father.

"We can certainly do that. But that will also finish the relationship you have with your husband. There will be no reconciliation after that. Don't forget that this is a male-dominated society. Think about it for a little more time. When you come back the second time, we will do as you say," he said.

That afternoon, we stopped by to have coffee at a cafeteria near Mum's uncle's office.

"So, what's the problem, Maa? We need Joy back."

"Yes, we need him back. I need to think the right course of action. Give me some time. Let me think."

"You are always so confused, Maa. Why do you take so much time to make decisions?" I argued back.

"Lismun, that's how life is. There is no black, there is no white. It is something in between."

Losing Joy was painful beyond tolerance. The pain pierced inside me like a sharp glass wedged between my foot and the ground.

The worst part was we did not know the end of it. And yet, Mum was in two minds about pressing charges against my father for abducting Joy. I never understood why the strongest woman on earth always walked nervously when it came to him.

Mum and I spent the whole weekend at home. There was no talk, no complaint, nothing. At least, we weren't arguing and for a change, the silence felt good.

Finally, Mum announced that she wasn't going to file a case against my father.

During summer vacation that year, my father took Joy to his aunt's place. Somehow, he thought that it was okay to leave his five-year old son with his uncle and aunt in a remote village. They were in their seventies and their family was into farming. Joy had never met them before, yet he spent forty days of his summer vacation with them. I wondered why my father didn't keep Joy with him. Maybe, he didn't have the guts to take care of a little boy; maybe, he just wanted Mum to become a subdued wife. We didn't know what his intentions were.

Mum managed to find out my father's cousin's phone number, and she talked to him about it.

"I don't know why Chaka left Joy at our uncle's place," he said.

"I don't know either. Maybe this is his way of mentally torturing me," Mum replied.

"My sympathies are with you, Nina. But he is a sadist. I am just appalled that he doesn't think about Joy at all. We always thought the little boy was his favorite in the family. I don't know what to say. Human beings are unpredictable, you know. Is there anything I can do for you?"

"Yes. I do need a favor from you."

"Tell me."

"Will you please go and meet Joy and tell me how he is doing?" Mum started to cry profusely.

"I will go and see him next week."

And he did. When he came back after spending a couple of days with Joy, I sensed that things weren't good.

He asked Mum and me to sit down at the dining table and continued, "I am going to be honest with you. Your son has become introverted and has lost weight. I can't believe how five months have changed him. He is just scared and anxious. He hardly talked to me when I went to meet him. I don't know how to say it, like he is alert and vigilant. He finds it hard to fall asleep in the night, and even if he manages to sleep after a lot of tossing and turning, he wakes up in the middle of the night, screaming and all sweaty. He talks about going back home. He has two toys to play with and he clings to them."

"I want to see my child," Mum began to cry uncontrollably.

"Go and see him. You will feel good and Joy will like it, too. Chaka goes there only during the weekends. Do something about it, Nina."

Mum looked at me.

"Don't talk to me," I said, "You have created this situation and I refuse to be a part of it."

"Just because I am looking at you does not mean I have something to say, Lismun," Mum answered back irritated.

"You are always mad at me. Why?" I replied with an angry face.

Mum and I didn't talk for the whole day. It was the first time I felt good not talking to her. I felt awkward and sad, because she didn't do what she needed to do to get Joy back. Instead, she sulked all the time. Her melancholic face and red eyes annoyed me, but I decided not to fight because it didn't make sense.

I refused to go with Mum to see my brother during the summer vacation. Mum dropped me at Grandpa's house and she headed to the village to meet my brother. She spent around five days with him. My father was out in another town for an official tour and it worked out well. Mum wrote me a long letter from there about how she was ecstatic about being with him. Mum also wrote that unfortunately, my father's aunt had severe knee pain and she couldn't play with Joy or cook food for him, but she was loving. Mum wrote that she took Joy to the fields in the evenings. I read that letter and threw it in the trash.

Grandpa asked me, "Lisa, you should treasure the letters written to you. You don't throw them away."

"Why shouldn't I? Maa is never happy with me and then she goes to meet Joy and sends me a letter."

"Your mother has her own struggles. Try to be kinder."

I was too angry to respond. Mum came back after a day. The first thing she said was, "I had a good time with Joy." And I hated it. It made me feel so insignificant, like she only loved Joy and I didn't matter.

That night Mum said, "I told him many interesting stories, but he didn't seem interested. No matter what I did, he refused to come out of his shell. All my questions were answered in mono-syllables."

"I don't care what he said or what he did. I don't want to know how you spent your time, Maa," I snapped.

Mum went back to being depressed again. It didn't matter that we were at my grandpa's place. She cried every night and I cried with her. Dark clouds had covered the skies above us and it didn't matter whether we were in Rampur or with my grandparents. No light could escape from those thick, stubborn, black clouds and there was nothing to look forward to!

I often wondered if there was another world inside earth, like some place underground where I could enter anytime from anywhere. I wished there was a place that would soak up all the darkness and troubles of my life, a place that would magically erase all my bad memories, so I could eventually become free and happy.

One afternoon when I was cleaning my room, Mum offered to help me out, but in the middle of it, she started to weep.

I told her, "I am tired of all this. Why don't you go and report this whole thing to the police?"

"I can't."

"Why not? What's wrong with you, Maa?"

"I don't know. I can't report it to the police. What if he takes Joy away? What if he kills us? I am going to be honest. I am not sure how the police would handle all this."

"Then do me a favor. Stop crying. What's the point of crying when you are not willing to do anything about it?"

"I am undecided. I can't think straight. We live in a society that is totally screwed up."

"Maa, the society is screwed up because of people like you."

"How dare you talk to me like that? I am your mother!"

Mum stormed out of the room. I rose from the sofa and shut the door. It was the first time I had talked back to her in such a rude way. But I was in no mood to apologize.

I knew Mum was not thinking about me. It wasn't fair. I missed Joy and I knew Mum missed him much more than I did. But to me, her behavior and explanations had no logic, no rhyme. I was mad and confounded and couldn't solve the puzzle. Maybe she had her own reason, maybe she was scared of the consequences, or maybe she feared the fake society around her. But I felt like I didn't exist for her and that feeling was tearing me up from inside.

A week later, on a Sunday morning, Mum announced, "I am going to see Joy again. I will leave tonight. You will be fine here at Grandpa's place, Lismun."

"I don't care what you do."

Mum bought clothes, sweets, toys, and lots of books. I knew Mum well, and I knew that she never believed in extravagance, so I was totally surprised to see her spend so much money.

"Why have you bought so many things, Mum? Do you think Joy is going to use all these?"

"All these things are not for Joy. There are lot of kids there who work on the farms and rice fields. Thought of taking a few things for them, too."

Mum left that evening and I stayed back at my grandparents' house. What Mum said that morning had a profound effect on me. I thought about it all the time.

So, Mum missed my brother, and our future was uncertain, yet she thought about the poor kids in the village.

That night when I played a board game with Grandpa, I asked him, "I think Mum seems to be really confused. Look at her. She cries all the time because she misses Joy and then she buys all these stuff for the poor kids in the village. She hardly has any new saree for herself."

Grandpa said, "Well, that's the thing about kindness. An act of kindness touches you no matter what you are going through, no matter what your situation, and no matter how you feel. Both parties feel good, the kind person and the person who benefits from it. Don't you think about it?"

It was profound for me, and I tried to let go of all the hatred and resentments I had harbored for Mum. I was mighty impressed with what Mum did. The last few days of my summer vacation at my grandparents' place were good. While Mum was gone, I spent time with Grandpa and Grandma. Grandma thought it was a good time to teach me how to make fried rice.

Mum spent four days with Joy during that visit, and he was glued to her. He loved to draw, just simple pencil drawings, and he spent hours drawing pictures of him and Mum.

When Mum came back after visiting him, we left for Rampur. And everything returned to where it was. The house was empty with just the two of us. Mum drowned herself in self-pity and tears, and I was left alone to fend for myself. We had no idea when my father took Joy back to the residential school and what happened after that. One night, Mum called Joy's school to speak to him and all she did was cry after hearing his voice.

I said to her calmly that night, "I want to be out of this place. It will not serve any purpose if you cry all the time like that, Mum. Tell me how exactly is your crying helping us."

Like most times, Mum chose to be silent and it frustrated me.

"I think you should send me to Grandpa's house. I will study there. Enroll me in a school in Sambalpur. Please, Maa," I pleaded.

But there was no answer. I was helpless to see Mum so weak emotionally. I saw her crumbling. My rock, my light was drowning in infinite grief that it was painful to watch. As Mum's daughter, I found it unbearable, so I begged Mum to take me to my grandparents' house.

"I told you earlier and I am telling you again. You can't go there because I need some love in my life. I can't live without both my kids."

And it was true, Mum certainly needed the love.

The good thing was that someone up there made sure about it. It seemed like Mum's prayers didn't go unanswered. Exactly one month later, my father had a terrible car accident and he was hospitalized. Mum decided to go see him and she took me along.

When we reached the hospital, my father was in the I.C.U., unconscious. He had nobody by his side, even though his parents and siblings had been informed about it.

Two days later, when he regained his consciousness and was able to talk, he looked at Mum and asked for forgiveness. He was bed ridden and needed help for his day to day activities. Mum offered to help, but she put a condition for him to bring Joy back. My father had no other option but to agree to it.

It was the beginning of fall semester of second grade for Joy's class. Since my father could not move from his bed, he asked one of his office colleagues, Mr. Roy, to go and get Joy. Mr. Roy worked under my father and held him on a high pedestal. I called him "Roy uncle." He treated Mum like a sister. He had raspy voice and intense, dark brown eyes. He cleared his throat before talking and always sounded funny. Sometimes, he bought candies for me and he would forget to tell me about it. I would find it later. But he was a great human being and was always there for us.

Mum decided to stay back with my father. She said, "You know I don't like that school. I will be a mess if I go there. You go with Roy uncle and get Joy."

My father called the School Principal, Mr. Tijori, and talked to him. He also wrote a letter for him.

Many years later, I found out the real reason why my mum stayed back that day. She didn't come with us because she didn't want my father to change his mind.

It was a weekend and I woke up early to board the bus with Roy uncle. When we reached at the residential school, I was excited and happy. I had saved some pocket money, so I bought few candy bars for Joy.

I was determined not to cry or become emotional. Once I saw Joy, I didn't say a word. I lifted him up, and he hugged me back. Roy uncle went out and wept. Joy wanted me to put him down. The moment I did, he ran out of the door to look for Mum.

"Maa is not here," I said.

"When will I see her?" he started to cry.

"You will see her today. We are here to take you home."

"Home? You mean, Rampur?"

"Yes."

But Joy ran away. I chased him.

"What happened? Aren't you happy that we are going home?"

"Why didn't Maa come? What's the point? I am coming back to this school again. I am not going anywhere. Tell Maa to come and meet me."

"Papa had an accident. Maa couldn't come because she is taking care of Papa. We are here to take you home, sweetie. We will take you home forever. Roy uncle is with me."

I can never forget his facial expression and his beautiful toothless smile. He sat on a chair and ate his candies while I dragged his half-broken suitcase from under the bed to pack his books and toys. I was happy, so was Joy, and we were going back home.

Our memory is like a copier machine. It copies everything, good or bad, and everything in between. I didn't have very many good days around that time, but the day we got Joy from the residential school was indeed a very special day. I still remember the checkered, blue shirt he was wearing and the brown slippers on his tiny feet.

Roy uncle was in the principal's office signing some papers. Once he came back, I had finished packing. There was chocolate all over Joy's face. He looked cute and funny. Roy uncle washed his face, held his hand, and we were out the door.

Roy uncle stopped by the principal's office to say goodbye. I was so angry just to see Mr. Tijori's face. I remember I turned towards him and said, "You never tried to find the truth. You didn't try to investigate what my father said was the true or not. You were wrong."

Roy uncle couldn't believe that I said those lines. He said, "Lisa, you should become a lawyer." We laughed about it!

As we headed home, Joy was happy that he would finally be able to show the drawings to Mum; all those priceless drawings he had created during his summer vacation away from her.

When we reached the hospital, Mum held him tight, and they cried for a long time; a sight glued to my mind. The reunion of Mum and Joy melted everyone's heart, an emotional poignancy that brought tears in all eyes. I stood in the corner and watched them. I could tell they had missed each other immensely.

When Joy was home with Mum, I spent the next day with Anna in a park close to our house.

She said, "Lisa, you are amazing. Look at you, it's like nothing breaks you."

I didn't say anything. I felt weak emotionally.

She continued, "I want to grow up quickly and I want to start work."

I looked at her and said, "I feel the same."

"Have you decided what you plan to do?"

"Not really."

"I love writing and maybe someday I will write for some newspaper."

"That sounds wonderful."

We walked for a long time that evening and ate cotton candy. I thanked God for that amazing friendship.

Chapter Twelve

Some Good Days....

After spending nearly two months in the hospital, my father was finally allowed to go back home. At home, he was mostly confined to bed. Mum hired a part-time cook to take care of us while she got busy taking care of my bedridden father.

We often ate dinner together. All of us were mostly quiet during dinner time. Mum tried to act as if nothing had happened. Nobody talked about what had happened to Joy. Nobody talked about his feelings and all the dirt was swept under the rug. I felt very confused during those days. But confusion did me good. It made my mind blank and I just focused on my studies.

In a couple of months when my father was finally able to walk on his own, he joined work. One morning, I saw my father making breakfast.

"Come sit down. Breakfast is almost ready," he said.

It became a daily routine for him to cook breakfast for me and Joy.

He wasn't overly affectionate, but he took care of us. But I remained a little wary. It was too good to be true.

One day, when I came back from school, I asked Mum, "Why is Papa behaving this way?"

"Like what?"

"Like being so nice and helping us out."

"People change. They realize their mistakes."

I couldn't believe Mum was so gullible. But I decided to be quiet. It was around the same time Mum decided to get a master's degree in education. Evenings became hectic. Mum often asked me to help Joy in his homework assignments. Fortunately, that was something I enjoyed.

Joy sat on my lap while we read books. I was six years older than him and he looked up to me. I taught him for an hour every day in the evening. I took him to the school playground to play. It was fun to giggle and talk about fire trucks, car engines, and motorbikes with my little brother.

My brother was the most beautiful kid I had ever seen. He was intelligent and very observant. He was reticent compared to me, but he adored me and listened to what I said. When he had doubts or homework questions he could not solve, he did not go to my father or mother, he came to me. I loved him and I loved him with all my heart.

One evening, all of a sudden, my father got mad about the way shampoo and conditioner bottles were arranged in the bathroom. And in just a few days, things turned back to where they were. The same cold treatment, passive aggressiveness, and extreme mood swings. We were back to square one. I was right, it was too good to be true.

My Father's Mother Died, March 1991

My father was the eldest of the four; he had two younger brothers and a sister. By 1991, his sister was married and had two kids of her own and she lived in a different city. My father's elder brother, Uncle Tola, lived near his parents' house. His youngest brother had finished college and lived with his parents and was looking for a job.

I hadn't spent a lot of time with my father's parents and didn't know them well. But they used to visit us once in a while and were nice to me and I was cordial to them.

In March 1991, my father's father had a heart attack and he was admitted in a hospital near Sambalpur. My father's mother stayed in his room to take care of him. She was fifty-six years old.

It was a weekday in the middle of March. My father was out of town on a business trip. Mum was sipping tea. I was watching T.V. and Joy was playing with his friends outside the house. Mum expected him to be back in the house as it was time for dinner. She looked outside of the window to see where he was.

The phone rang. Mum picked it up. It was Uncle Tola.

He said, "Maa is dead."

Mum's face changed immediately and she dragged a chair behind her to sit down. I ran and stood by her side. She just held my hand tightly.

"What?" Mum could hardly say anything else.

"Yes, our beloved mother is dead. We are taking her body to Sonepur. It would be nice if you come with us," he said.

"Yes. I will come with you all," Mum didn't even think twice before saying that.

That's all. That was the phone call. I ran outside to find Joy. He had parked his tiny bike somewhere in the woods. I couldn't find him. I looked for him little bit more and found him trying to climb a mango tree with some friends.

He refused to come with me because he was having too much fun. I held his bike in one hand and his hand in another while I dragged him out of there. He kept kicking and biting me. But I was way stronger than him.

Once we were home, Mum was almost ready. At that point, we didn't even realize that none of us had eaten. Joy wanted his dinner. Mum quickly packed some snacks for him.

I had not taken a shower, so I asked Mum for ten more minutes.

But Mum said, "We don't have time for a shower. Just change your clothes. We are leaving for Sonepur now."

"Why Mum? It will not take more than five minutes?" I argued.

"Because I told you so. Your grandmother died two hours back. Your uncle is coming here with her dead body. We have to go to Sonepur, so they can perform the rituals," Mum insisted.

In an hour or so, my uncle was in front of our house with her dead body in a rented van. He was there with his wife and his two daughters.

There were just two seats in the front row. Uncle Tola and the driver sat there, and we all sat behind. They had put the body at the back of the van. I was the one closest to it.

Joy was very scared and looked out of the window the whole time. Everyone was quiet. I looked outside for some time. Then I looked at the body. It just looked terrible. Her eyes were shut, her face looked cold, and sort of blue. The color of her skin was pale.

I felt sad and confused. I wasn't prepared to be with a dead body inside a closed, moving van for four hours.

I had to talk because I was feeling suffocated. Being silent in that situation was the last thing I wanted to do. Mum was holding our hands the whole time.

"Mum, why does she look blue?" I asked Mum

Mum responded quietly, "Because she is dead."

I had more questions to ask. But Mum gave me that look that meant I should be quiet, so I sat in silence. Once we reached Sonepur, there were lot of people to help us out with the body. As my father was still out of the town and his father was still in the hospital, everyone waited for them to be back to start the rituals.

They had put the body in the middle of the house's huge *veranda* for people to come and offer their condolences.

My father reached Sonepur after midnight. Mum and I were still awake, but Joy had fallen asleep. My father sat by the body and cried loudly. I fell asleep that night listening to his cries.

I woke up early the next morning and sat in one corner. I watched how family members from my father's side followed the rituals. Her body had been washed by some of her sisters with milk and yogurt. Some women poured purified water from Ganges to wash it for the final time. While washing, they were reciting mantras. Once they were done cleaning the body, her big toes were tied together. She was dressed in red as she died before her husband.

There were several small oil lamps lighted around her. Her head faced south. The village priest instructed the family members to prepare the body and dress her. They did exactly the way he wanted.

It was not unusual for Hindu people to keep the bodies in the house for eighteen or twenty hours after death prior to cremation. Once her body was cremated, my father and his brothers went to Ganges in the north of India to scatter her holy ashes.

It took my father and his brothers around five days to return. We stayed with my father's family while my father was gone. During that time, most of my father's distant relatives were good to us. My father's father was discharged from the hospital and he came home, too. My father's sister, who lived in a town little far from Sonepur, came and joined the mourning members of the family, too.

The rituals were performed for thirteen days after her death. Meanwhile, the food was being prepared at a neighbor's house. It was vegetarian, mostly plain white rice and lots of curries without many spices.

As more relatives started pouring in the house, Joy and I felt isolated. But it was still okay. Mum took care of us, heated the water for our showers, cooked for us. All this while my father, his father, his sister, and his younger brother weren't talking to Mum.

Uncle Tola and his wife were decent to Mum. They were polite and spoke respectfully. His wife sometimes waited for Mum to have lunch together. Sometimes Uncle Tola played with Joy.

Finally, all the relatives and neighbors were invited to have a meal that comprised all of my father's mother's favorite dishes and lots of sweets.

I looked at Mum and said, "When will we leave?"

"Maybe in a day or two," Mum wasn't sure.

"Do you think Papa will come with us?" I asked her.

"I am not sure," Mum said.

That night when we went to sleep, we heard my father and his father talking loudly. It was something about money. I was too sleepy to say anything, so I went to bed.

It was about two in the morning when Mum woke us up.

"Get up, Lismun. Get up right now."

"Mum, I am sleepy. We will talk tomorrow."

"We will not be here tomorrow morning. We have to leave now."

"What? Why, Maa? Why are we leaving now?"

"Because they want us to leave right now. Yes, now," Mum screamed.

Finally, when I sat up, Mum's eyes were full of fury. She looked like a tigress preparing to fight and her valor was commendable. I had never seen her like that in my entire life.

"Why do they want us to leave now? What's wrong? Where is Papa? Why can't he stand up for us once?" I asked Mum rubbing my eyes and trying to wake up fully.

"There is no reason. Why does your father abuse us? Why? Why did he kidnap Joy? There is no reason, Lisa. I am sorry, sweetie. I can't reason anymore. They told me after dinner that we had to leave, and we are leaving."

I packed some clothes and medicines in the room. Joy didn't have time to change.

When we came down, my father, his father, his siblings, and all their family members were gathered in the *veranda*. Mum picked up the suitcase, I carried a big bag, and we left from the front door. I looked back with tears flowing from my eyes.

Uncle Tola said, "It's still dark. Why should they go now?"

My father's father said, "They have to leave now. Right now."

My father didn't even look at us as we stepped out of the house. Mum kept walking. It was the first time I saw her angry, real mad. We got a taxi and went straight to the bus stop. The problem was that there was no bus so early in the morning, but the ticket counter was still open. Mum gave me the money to buy the tickets.

When I came back, I saw Mum sitting on a bench in one corner, Joy sleeping on her lap. I looked at them from a distance and just knew it was the "now or never" moment. I walked slowly and sat down by Mum's side without saying a word. I looked at her and found her looking at Joy, who was sleeping. Strangely, Mum didn't look mad anymore. She didn't look sad either.

Mum turned towards me and said, "Lismun, there is no fun in being a victim. I am tired of crying, and so are you kids. There is no fun in thinking about all the wrong doings of some of our relatives. Things need to change.

There will be new challenges. But we are going to thrive on those challenges. Now that will be fun, right?"

"What do you mean by that, Maa?" I said with irritation in my voice.

Mum continued, "Sitting here all alone with two kids, something struck me, and it struck me hard."

"I know, Maa. We have so many problems in our lives. They just don't stop. They keep pouring from all directions."

"How would someone muster courage to throw his daughter-in-law and her kids out of the house in the middle of the night? How did that happen? This is a realization for me. How did I let things come this far? Why did I have to go there when I wasn't wanted?" Mum kept talking without paying attention to whether I was listening or not, as if she was talking to herself.

"I am so mad. I am angry at my myself. I am sad and I feel broken," Mum continued. "Look at me! I am here at the bus stop with two school going kids. Enough is enough. I am the only person who can change the situation," she said with anger floating in her eyes.

That night, to a great extent, I knew how Mum felt. She had given what I thought were lame excuses all my growing up years; sometimes, it was society, sometimes, it was her being a single mother, and sometimes, money. She always had a flickering hope that someday, somehow a miracle would happen and things would change. It never happened. In the whole process, she got many big jolts, but she waited and she waited.

But this time, Mum fell straight on her face and she hit the ground hard, very hard. All she had now was us and her failing courage. When I was a little girl, Mum always consoled me after every fight that things would become okay. But our situation worsened with every passing year.

"I had told you to send me to Grandpa's house. Your problems would have been less without me, I think," I said, as if I was sorting things in my head.

"I don't know what else I could have done. But this is where my patience ends."

I had never heard Mum talk like that. But I was too tired to say anything. My eyes were drooping. My body and muscles ached with exhaustion. I wasn't sure what she meant, but it sure was a sign that things needed to change.

"What's the time now, Maa?"

"Three-thirty in the morning."

"The ticket counter people told me that the bus will be here to board passengers at six. I will sleep for some time," I said while leaning back against the wall and with my eyes closed.

I fell asleep fast, but Mum woke me up.

"Wake up, Lismun."

"What's up with you, Maa? I am tired… Don't you see it? I am a child and I don't understand what adults do. Let me sleep. Please, Maa."

"I have made my decision," Mum said

"Let me sleep, Maa," I was begging her now.

"We will move out," Mum said.

"What?" I woke up immediately.

Mum didn't say anything else and I didn't ask as I boarded the bus with Mum and Joy. I had a throbbing headache. We sat in the back seat of the bus, and it was bumpy ride.

We were tired and sleep deprived, but our eyes weren't empty, and still had dreams in some corners.

"If we live separately, will we still live in the same town as Papa?" I asked.

"I don't think so," Mum said.

"Then?"

"We will move in with Grandpa and Grandma. You will go to school in Sambalpur."

"I will like that, Maa."

"I feel strange, Lismun. I feel strong and at the same time, I feel weak. I am scared of what the future holds for us, but I can't do more than this. I need to walk out of all this for you and Joy. I could never figure out what he really wanted. I gave my very best. But this is where it ends."

Mum had made her decision. I was happy and hopeful that there would be light at the end of the tunnel. After that bus journey of four hours, things changed; the way we perceived things, our dreams, and our goals. Everything changed *for the better*.

Once we were back in Rampur, the first thing Mum did was to look for job openings in Sambalpur. She sent applications to as many schools as she could. "I have some interviews coming up," she said, "I have already talked to Grandpa. We will move in with them."

Once Mum's job was confirmed, she had fifteen days to join. The biggest challenge for Mum was to uproot us from school. I was finishing up eighth grade and Joy was finishing up second grade. We had another six weeks of school left. After thinking about it for a couple of days, Mum decided not to wait.

Chapter Thirteen

My Last Day of School in Rampur

My father was still in his parents' house when we moved out. Grandpa came to help us with a mini truck to take our belongings. Although we didn't have a lot of stuff, Mum left a couple of beds and some furniture there. I decided to take my study desk and chair. Joy took some of his toys and Mum packed the kitchen utensils and our clothes.

Before we left, Grandpa asked me to go to my school and say goodbye to everyone. I hugged Pali and Anna. I told I would write to them regularly. Anna cried profusely. Pali said that I was always going to be her best friend.

After meeting the school principal and some more teachers, I went to meet Mr. Sharma for the last time.

It was lunchtime and he was eating.

"May I come in?" I asked.

He looked at me and said, "Don't you see it is lunchtime now? I can't talk to you."

"Yes, sir. I know it is lunchtime. I am leaving the school today for good. Mum is moving to a different place. I just wanted to say something to you before I leave."

"What is it? You have one minute. Speak."

I walked up to his desk, looked straight into his eyes, and said, "You tried hard to break my spirit. But you couldn't. I stand tall today and always will."

I finished my sentence and walked out of the door. I didn't wait to see his reaction. I am not sure what he felt or what he did after that. But I felt great in a way I had never experienced before. I sang that day with happiness as I walked home from school. The determination I felt inside me was unmatched.

Once we finished loading all our stuff in the truck, I looked back at the house where we had lived for so many years. It was painful but liberating. I sat in the tiny lawn in front of our house and cried for an hour.

For all my life, I had thought I was trapped in that situation and there was no end to it, but now, I was finally leaving.

For once in my life, I cried not because of pain, but because I had started to build hopes and dreams. That feeling was out of this world.

Initially, I had plans of leaving a letter for my father, but his response to Mum changed my mind. When Mum called him on the phone, he said, "Do whatever you want. I don't care."

I decided not to leave any letter or note for him. Mum gave away some clothes and old furniture to our neighbor's maid. As we started our three hours long journey to Sambalpur, I sat near the window in the truck and the wind on my face felt refreshing. Birds flying up in the sky, people selling stuff in their shops, and kids jumping in the water puddle by the roadside meant so much to me. I was full of dreams as I waved at them.

We stopped by at a small restaurant to eat dinner.

Mum asked me, "Lismun, you know I am saving for your undergraduate studies?"

I wasn't expecting a question like that from her, but she looked pretty darn serious.

"Yes, Maa. I know."

"You have to tell me whether you want me to spend it on your education or on your marriage, whatever little money I have."

"Spend it on my education."

Mum didn't say anything but smiled lightly as if she had anticipated that answer from me.

"Wait a minute, you have saved some money?" I asked.

"Yes, I have. Very little. I have been saving since the day you were born. Finally, we will live without chaos."

I couldn't agree more. Mum had tried her best. She had given her sweat, tears, and blood to make the relationship work. But now the drama, the painfully annihilative nights, days filled with tears and humiliation, moments that dismantled the courage piece by piece were all over!

Chapter Fourteen

My Grandfather's Palatial House and My High School Days, A New Chapter of My Life, April 1991

I was thirteen and Joy was seven when Mum moved in with her parents. When we were unpacking, Mum said, "I am glad I don't have to walk on the eggshells here." And she didn't.

My grandpa had a big house in Sambalpur. Aunt Renu called it "Grandpa's palatial house." It had two floors and was more than three thousand square feet. I loved the big windows and the book shelves. The house was slightly old styled though, with tall ceilings. There was a big terrace and we fell in love with it.

I began my freshman year of high school in fall of 1991. I liked the school. Kids were good, teachers were good. The only disadvantage was that the school was way too far from home at the other end of the city.

Mum was genuinely happy. She had varieties of interests. She kept herself busy. She stitched clothes, she cooked, painted, and did a lot of gardening in her spare time.

I loved hanging out with my grandparents, too. They were very affectionate towards us. I really loved the milk tea Grandma made. I devoured it every time with all my heart.

The problem was that Mum had very little money. Mum was an elementary school teacher and promotions in her school were seldom given. But the biggest challenge was that many teachers were employed by the state government weren't given their salaries regularly. They received their salaries, three-four times in a year. So, when Mum got the money, she got it in bulk but even then, she hardly had cash in her hand because she was saving it for us.

One morning, when I was waiting for the school bus, Mum came running, "Lismun, you forgot your lunch box."

"Thanks, Maa!" I said.

My school bus had a flat tire and it was delayed for an hour. As we waited for the bus, Mum opened up to me about the money situation.

"I feel very guilty about not being able to contribute towards the house expenses," she said looking at the busy road.

"I understand, Maa. But don't fret about this. We have been through hell and survived. We will be fine."

"I know," Mum smiled.

Even though I was only thirteen, I was Mum's best friend. There were many things I told her on a regular basis, "It will be all right,", "Don't worry," to encourage her. I knew my words gave Mum a lot of strength. But I was a mess deep inside and nobody had an inkling about it.

Amidst all the moves and changing school, I found the first couple of months difficult to adjust. My ability to think straight was severely impaired. I had a hard time getting used to the normal life. I often had nightmares in the night and woke up crying.

One night, I woke up screaming because I saw someone killing me. When Grandma came running inside my room, she found me shivering and covered with sweat. When she held me tight, all I could say was, "Papa will kill all of us. I know he will."

She was shocked to see how scared I was. That's why she slept in my room for the next three weeks. Grandpa stepped in to help me, too, just like in the good old days. By 1991, Grandpa was retired and had lots of time on his hands. A couple of weeks later, when I came back from school, Grandpa was waiting for me.

"Lisa, eat some snacks. We will go for a walk," he said with a sweet smile.

As we walked that evening, I enjoyed the chirping of birds and the different shapes of clouds made in the sky.

"It feels like old days, Grandpa. I remember how you used to carry me in your arms when I was a little girl and you were working in Balangir."

"Yes, those were good days, Lisa."

"So much have happened between then and now, Grandpa," I said.

"Yeah. True. But I know that you grew up stronger mentally with time. Let's focus on the chirping of the birds. Can we?"

"Yes, Grandpa."

"Tell me what bird is making that sound."

"Come on, that's a crow."

"Yes, crows sing well."

"You must be kidding. Cuckoos sing well, not crows."

We both started to laugh.

"Question for you, Grandpa. What's a herd of crows called?"

"I don't know."

"Murder."

We walked for another mile or so before coming back home. It was bliss and that's what I needed to refresh my mind before my tests. Those evening walks refreshed my mind whenever I was tired.

High School, Sambalpur

Even though my spirits were down, I loved my new school. During the first few months, I was mostly quiet and kept to myself. But in my heart of hearts, I wanted friends, just simple people. Like a normal child, I wanted to be surrounded by kids who would just listen to me and not judge me.

I took my time to settle down in my freshman year. I observed everyone closely. I had to do it to protect my own self. I got lucky. Two of the girls that I started hanging out were Minu and Annie. We ate our lunch together and sat on the same long bench during classes. It was funny because all three of us spoke different languages at home. I was boisterous, and I did not have an iota of fear to say what I felt and expressed my thoughts on politics, world problems, and class courses. Annie was shy and reticent. She spoke very few words. Minu was the most mature among us. She always knew when to talk and what to say.

At home, things had stabilized a lot. There were less sad days and fewer tears. But things took a bad turn when my father got posted in Sambalpur towards the end of 1991. He lived on the other side of town, very close to my school. My biggest fear was that he would show up in my school suddenly. I was so paralyzed with that fear that I threw up every day in school after lunch all of ninth grade.

One weekend, when some of us met at a friend's place for group study, I saw him near a grocery store. He had long hair and a beard. The moment I saw him, I hid behind a tree and refused to participate in the group. I wasn't sure if he saw me.

A month later, he showed up at my grandparents' house. It was a warm Sunday afternoon. Mum and Joy were taking afternoon *siestas* after a heavy lunch. My grandpa was out of the house. I sat on the stairs, munching a green guava when I heard the doorbell ring. I opened the door and it was my father.

"Oh, Hello, Papa." I shivered.

"Where is your maa? Call her."

"Maa is sleeping. I will call her right away. Please come inside the house."

"No, I don't want to go inside."

My grandma heard us talking and came out, "Oh, Chaka. Come inside the house."

"No. I will wait here."

By now, Mum had come out of the house, too, "Let's talk inside the house."

"No, I will not come inside."

"What is that you want to talk about?" Mum asked him.

"I want to let you know that the consequences of moving to Sambalpur will be bad," my father was screaming at the top of his voice now.

I saw a neighbor had opened her window and was peeping through to see the drama going on outside our house.

"Well, you didn't give us much choice. Did you?" Mum said angrily.

My father was livid with anger now, he kicked the door.

"Stop kicking the door. This is my parents' house. You can't do all this here," Mum looked mad.

He was gone even before Mum could finish her sentence. He vanished within minutes.

I cried a lot after my father left. Things took a reverse turn at that point of time. It set me right back emotionally where I had started from and I had a long uphill battle to fight.

When my grandpa came back in the evening, he said, "Don't worry about it, Lisa. Everything will be fine."

Mum assured me that I was safe, but my scars were too deep. No matter how much my grandparents showered their love, I found it impossible to bounce back. My feelings of abandonment and helplessness overwhelmed me every night.

There were constant fears in my head that there was someone out there to kill us, that Joy had been kidnapped again, and I would be separated from Mum. Those thoughts in my subconscious created havoc in my mind. I dreaded going to sleep in the night because I was afraid of the dark. I developed a habit of going to bed with the lights on.

My self-confidence was at all-time low. I was also very confused. One moment, I was voluble and talked a lot. Next moment, I couldn't speak at all.

I felt a void in my life that I found it hard to express in front of anyone. I tried to keep myself positive with good thoughts by reading books and diverting my mind, but it really didn't work long term.

Tears were my constant companion. I would start crying in the middle of the class for no apparent reason, or I would throw a tantrum at home out of nowhere.

One evening, Mum made my favorite egg noodles. I was so upset because it was slightly spicy that I took the whole plate and threw it against the wall. Needless to say, that upset Mum and she slapped me across the face. Mum had spanked me earlier but never on the face. She had tears in her eyes.

"I don't want to live," it was all that I could say at that moment.

I needed glasses for my eyes. I looked different from other girls and I liked it that way. *New school, new looks, life will be okay*, I told myself. But no matter what I did, the constant fear of abandonment overwhelmed me. I wondered what I would do if Mum left me or my grandparents threw me out of the house.

One Sunday, I was quiet, very quiet. I spent my morning and afternoon in my room without talking to anyone or eating my meals. Grandpa came to check on me. He said, "It is okay to be quiet. But know that I am here for you anytime you want to talk."

"I feel so angry about everything around me. I don't know why. I don't know how to make myself happy. I want to be calm but there are moments when I feel mad about everything, I see around me," I said in an irritated tone.

"I know. I understand how you feel, Lisa."

I looked at him. He smiled back. As he walked out of my room, he left the door ajar in case I changed my mind. And I did. I ate dinner with everyone that night. It felt wonderful.

If I had exams and I was burning the midnight oil, he sat by my side reading a newspaper. That made a profound impact on me. Just to see him like that, every day, every hour, and every second.

It did not take me long to realize that Mum had inherited her mental strength and determination from her father.

Soon, I realized that things weren't easy for Grandpa either. Mum's elder brother, Uncle Bhanja, had become a chain smoker. When he came to visit my grandparents for a few days with his family, he looked lost and smoked all the time. And then there was Mum who had moved in with them with two kids.

One of those days, I saw my grandpa come out of the bathroom with watery red eyes. I knew he cried in the bathroom. But when he was with us, he laughed and joked. I was touched by his ability not to let the sadness in his life win his emotions.

What amazed me the most was, his ability to remain happy at all time. His ability to find joy in small things was so powerful that everything else looked blurred.

He appreciated Mum and Grandma after every meal, no matter what they had cooked and how bad the food tasted. He lived his life by being an example. Not by telling others what to do. To me, his stature was taller than Mount Everest and his strength was deeper than any ocean. His courage was overwhelming at times, as if he feared nothing, as if he were ready for anything that life threw at him.

During my sophomore year of high school, we had many rounds of debate competitions. During the final round, as I stood there and talked about civil rights, I saw my grandpa sitting in the last row in the audience. He wasn't wearing his glasses, his face was covered with sweat, and he was crying. He showed me a thumbs up

Once the results were announced, I got the first prize. I took my trophy and sat down with him. He smiled and showed me another thumbs up. He said, "You were good up there."

We both hugged and cried. He was seventy-five years old. We didn't have a car. He rode his bicycle for nearly fifteen miles, from one end of town to another end to come and watch me talk. That was priceless.

I had a strange feeling that night and I suddenly felt that eventually things would work out. I realized to some extent, if not completely, that my fears of abandonment were baseless.

Mum constantly reminded me how grateful we should be that my grandparents were taking care of us.

"They have done a lot for us. I don't know how to pay them back?" Mum said one night.

Next morning, when we were eating breakfast, Mum told Grandpa, "I don't know how we can repay for all your help."

"Parents have unconditional love for their kids. You don't have to do anything for us," he said.

But Mum was the last person on earth to take help from people, even from her own parents. In the next few weeks, Mum figured out a way to resolve her guilt feelings.

I couldn't be happier for two reasons. First, she stopped bugging me about how to repay my grandparents and second, she set another example for me to see how we could show our gratitude towards people without paying them money.

Mum saved her salary for us and contributed little money for the household expenses and didn't pay any rent. But she compensated for it well. She cooked, cleaned, and took care of everything in the house. It all worked out smoothly because there was a silent understanding between Mum and her parents.

She told to me, "I will take care of these two people during their old age." And she kept her promise.

That was new chapter in our lives. Mum worked hard and that inspired me. She got up early in the morning at five. She cooked breakfast and lunch for everyone. Once we left for school around eight-thirty, she cleaned the house and left for work around nine. Evenings were easier, but there were always guests at home, relatives from Grandpa's or Grandma's family.

Mum liked entertaining the guests. I wasn't sure why she liked working hard and pleasing my grandparents' distant relatives. Maybe it took her mind off other problems. Maybe she wanted to connect with them as my father had kept her isolated, far away from her relatives.

With time, I settled down, too. I was okay, if not great. I still got nightmares, I still cried, and I still felt depressed, but I spent a lot of time reading books. My favorite books were Mark Twain's The Adventures of Huckleberry Finn and The Adventures of Tom Sawyer, Eric Segal's Love Story, and Jeffry Archer's Prodigal Daughter.

We had a good library in our school from which I borrowed books every week. Grandpa appreciated my growing love for literature. On my fifteenth birthday, he took me book shopping and bought Charles Dickens' Oliver Twist, A Tale of Two Cities, and Great Expectations.

"Thank you, Grandpa. This is the best gift I have ever received in my life."

"You are welcome," he said with the brightest smile on his face.

Grandma was an introvert. She spoke less, but that didn't stop her from bragging about me or pampering me. My wish was her command as far as food was concerned. Sometimes, I exasperated her with my constant demand for *chai*, Indian tea. I never liked plain milk but tea made with whole milk was something I loved. So, Grandma had a big mug of hot tea ready for me when I returned home from school.

For my grandparents, life had come full circle. Joy and I filled their empty house with our giggles and sweet voices. It was lively and vivacious! They lived very simple lives, yet they provided abundance of love to me and my brother. But the best thing, they did was respect us. They never imposed anything on us. They didn't force us to adhere to any norm.

One thing troubled me. People in Sambalpur didn't know anything about my father. I struggled emotionally when people asked me, "What does your father do?"

Though it was a normal question, I dreaded it. Most times, I didn't answer anything. I didn't know how to cope with all my emotions, but I had learned how to program my mind and control my thought process if not completely but to a large extent. My thoughts controlled my mental state. That was the bottom line. There was no way I was going to dwell in my past and feed my negative thoughts—I told this to myself every morning.

My Room

Our Sambalpur house had steps that connected the kitchen to the bedroom. I often sat there. There was a house being constructed in the open lot on the left side of our house and the constant noise gave me a throbbing headache. Grandpa came and sat by my side as I was sipping tea and smiled at me. I smiled back, painfully though.

"Lisa, this is your home. There are six bedrooms, pick whichever you want as your room," he said softly.

I looked back at his smiling face. That's exactly what I needed; kindness and love.

"I will take the last room that faces the street. I like it because it has big windows."

"Fine, it is yours," he declared.

My brother picked his room, too, opposite to mine. He was too scared to sleep on his own, so he would sneak into Mum's room in the night. I guess that's how Mum liked it, too.

I loved my room. It wasn't spacious, but it wasn't small either. I had a full-sized bed in my room and my old study desk. I arranged the furniture and kept it clean. There was still enough space on the floor to put a mat and sit down. I liked it that way. Simple and beautiful. I knew I was home. For me, all the gray clouds were gone and there was sun. Bright and sunny. Everything looked good. Days were warm and nights had starry skies. Things looked promising. But most of all, there was peace.

Chapter Fifteen

Sona!

In my freshman year of high school, Grandma hired a part-time maid. Her name was Sona. She was eighteen years old. She was tall, of medium build, and had light brown eyes. She loved clothes, jewelry, and tied her hair in a ponytail. She was particular about how she looked. She was beautiful, and she knew it.

Sona worked in two other houses during the day and mostly came to our house during the evenings. As I was home most evenings, I got to know her well.

Sona's job was to mop the floors in every room, dust the wooden furniture, and fold the washed clothes. She was punctual and never missed a day of work.

One day as I ate my dinner, she cleaned the floor. She cleaned it so well that the cement floor reflected light.

"Wow, you have done an amazing job!" I told her.

"I like it that way," she said with pride.

"Like what? Like so shiny that it reflects light?"

"It is more than that. I like to do my job well."

"So nice of you to say it, Sona."

She smiled and went back to mopping the floor. I continued looking at her in awe. I couldn't believe how fast she cleaned and how hard she worked. She was just a few years older than me.

"You are so hard working, Sona," I said.

"I don't have an option. I have so many responsibilities on me."

"Responsibilities? What responsibilities? You are just eighteen!"

"Eighteen is a big number. You have to be good at what you do."

With time, Sona became a good friend. When she came to clean our house in the evening, my room was the last one she cleaned. She looked forward to talking to me, and I loved listening to her stories.

"So, what do you learn in school?" she asked me one evening.

"I learn about everything."

"Give me some examples."

"Well, I learn how to write poems and stories. I learn how to do calculations. We read books about Maharajas and their queens. A lot of stuff around us, science, places in the world, geography."

"Very nice."

"Sona, tell me something. Did you ever go to school?"

"Yes, I did."

She paused for a couple of seconds, then said, "I had to stop school after 5th Grade."

"Oh, that's bad. Why did you stop then?"

"I will tell you that story some other day," she flashed her brightest smile as she left my room.

Mum was very appreciative of what Sona did for us and paid her well, almost double the money Sona made in other houses.

Mum had established a routine of cooking breakfast and lunch before work. She cooked dinner after work every evening. If there was any leftover, Mum saved it for Sona and her family. If Mum made something delicious, she never forgot to set aside a big share for her. Sona thanked Mum for her generous heart and left no stone unturned to keep Mum happy. In just a few months, Sona had become a member of our family. We all loved her dearly.

Sona was an amazing girl and was quite outgoing by nature. As time passed, I started to feel that Sona was more like a friend or sister. I trusted her completely and she had access to everything in my room. I offered to teach her if she was willing to learn. She told me she would think about it.

Every once in a while, I got pocket money from Grandpa, not much, just enough to buy candy bars or sandwiches from the school cafeteria. To me, it was a substantial amount of money. I always left the money on my study table drawer and never thought much about it.

After few weeks, I discovered a peculiar pattern. I found that the money disappeared on a regular basis. I knew Joy had no interest in my money. I suspected it was Sona. But the last thing I wanted to do was to ask her without proof. Also, I wanted to solve this problem on my own without involving the adults.

I decided to change the place where I kept the money. One day after school, I requested Sona to get tea and I went to take a shower. When I came out of the bathroom, I saw the steaming hot cup of tea placed on my table. Sona was frantically looking for something in my room. She was searching under the pillows, between the books on the shelves, and under the bedsheet. I stood near the door without saying a word.

When she turned back, she froze with embarrassment.

I smiled at her and gave a hug and asked her calmly, "What are you looking for?"

"Your tea is on the table," she could barely manage to speak because of nervousness and walked out of the door.

"Wait, Sona. We need to talk," I said.

"I have to go home. I have to cook," she disappeared.

The next day was Saturday. There was a river behind our house, and I loved collecting stones on the bank of the river. We had half a day school every Saturday. Once I was done with my homework, I picked up my khaki bag, blue backpack and I was off to the river side to collect stones.

Once I got tired of gathering stones, I sat under the shade of a big, banyan tree and saw a small hut made of up big wooden sticks, dead tree branches, and thick clothes. I heard screams coming out from there. I thought someone needed help, so I ran.

When I entered inside, I found out it was Sona's house. Her father and mother had held her long hair tight and she was on the ground screaming as they punched and kicked her. For a second, I thought it was a bad dream. But it was real, as real as it could be. They were hitting her so hard that I cried loudly, "Stop it. Stop it right now!"

But they didn't. I took a cooking pan from the side and hit her father on his back. He fell down. I hit him again, this time his leg. Sona found courage when she saw me fighting for her. She got up, grabbed the pan from my hand, and was about hit her mum when I shouted, "Not on the head, not on the head."

She paid heed to what I said and hit her mum on the right leg. I pushed her mother to the ground. Sona held my hand tight and we ran out of the house. We ran straight for five minutes without speaking a word. I had to stop because I was gasping for air.

Sona bled from her mouth. As we sat on the sandy banks of the river, Sona looked up at the sky and said, "Do you know how many more days we have for full moon?"

At that moment, I thought she was the craziest person on earth to ask me a weird question like that.

"I don't know. Maybe a couple of days. Why are you asking?"

"I need to arrange money for Raj."

"Who is Raj?"

"My boyfriend."

"You have a boyfriend? You never told me that."

"There is nothing to talk about him."

"I don't understand all this, Sona. You need to tell me everything. Why don't you want to talk about your boyfriend? Why were your parents beating you like that?"

"Yes, I have a boyfriend, and I don't talk about him because he gives me more pain than happiness. He expects money from me every full moon."

"And you give it to him?"

"Yes."

"Why? You are his girlfriend, not his slave."

"I have no option. He beats me if I don't give him money."

"This is crazy. Have you ever told your parents about it?"

"Yes. But what difference does it make? They beat me up, too. You saw it today. My boyfriend drinks and so do my parents. I am their slave. They fight with each other and they fight with me."

"Forget about your boyfriend for a second…but your parents. Now, that part is so confusing. Why do they treat you like that? Why?"

"They are both the same. They drink throughout the day and stay at home. How can they work when they are under the influence of alcohol day in and day out? And then they expect me to bring money and feed them. Sometimes, they send me for buying liquor in the night."

"So, they have never worked?"

"They did when I was little. But once I was ten or so, my mother left her job as a maid and sent me instead. Then my father left his job as a laborer. They stayed home and had nothing to do and got bored. I don't know how it all started. They started drinking in moderate amount in the beginning, and then it became worse with time. I was always there, so it was easy for them to make me their target. I met my boyfriend at a wedding. He lives close by. I thought he loved me, but he turned out to be the same. They are all the same."

I hugged her and took her near the water to wash her wounds. Seeing the blood-soaked water dripping from her mouth made me angry.

"How can they do it to you?"

"What's the big deal about it? My parents have been abusing me since I was a little girl. I was never good enough for them."

I sat there for a long time with Sona that evening. Our stories were so similar, yet so different. I didn't have a boyfriend and had no intention of having one, so that was good. I was grateful that at least I had one parent by my side.

I looked at Sona with teary eyes and said, "I am so glad I have Mum by my side. She fights for me."

That made her even sadder and she sobbed.

"I know your mother loves you," she said in a whispering voice.

"I am sorry if I hurt you, Sona."

"No, you didn't, Lisa. I have been meaning to tell you... I steal your money every week. I am the culprit and you can give me any punishment you want."

"I knew it all along," I said as I wiped her tear.

"You did? Why didn't you tell me? Does your mum know?"

"I didn't ask you because I was hoping you would tell me the truth. As far as Mum is concerned, no, she has no idea about it."

"I will return it as soon as I can."

"You don't have to, Sona. Forget about it."

"What will you say to your mum about it?"

"Nothing. It was my pocket money that Grandpa gave me. Maa is not going to ask me about it."

"Will you forgive me?"

"Yes, I forgive you right now."

We sat there for a long time, throwing stones in the river, and watching them make ripples on the still water. I don't know what Sona thought but I had countless thoughts, like those ripples circling around my mind that evening, *What would I have done if Mum were like Sona's mother?*

Sona and I went home late that evening. When we reached home, it was past eight. Mum was standing near the front gate and look worried.

"Where were you the whole day? You haven't eaten anything. Aren't you hungry? Your school bag is still lying in the living room. What's going on?" Mum asked me with a worried face.

"I was busy doing more important things than eating food or putting my bag on the table."

Mum smiled, "And what is that thing?"

"I was with Sona. She will stay with us for a few days. I hope you don't have any problem with that."

"Sure, she can stay here for a few days. She is most welcome. It can't be permanent though," Mum was clear about it.

Even though we had many spare rooms in the house, Sona slept in my room. Mum gave her a good mattress that she put on the floor. She went to sleep around ten in the night.

I asked her, "I study in the night and will have to have the lights on. Is that okay?"

"Yes, that's fine. You do what you are supposed to do," she said softly.

Joy and the New School

Joy was never thrilled to go to school. Even when he was in preschool in Rampur, he would make a huge fuss about going. Mum had given a big box of small candies to his teacher. And the teacher gave him one every day in the morning, which helped. But when we moved to Sambalpur, he was still hesitant. I had always loved learning no matter what, so I couldn't figure out why Joy didn't like his new school.

During my junior year, Grandpa bought me a beautiful, blue bike with pink handles. The only condition was that I had to clean it every week, which I did diligently. One evening, when I was washing my bike with soapy water, Joy came and sat by side. He wasn't one of those kids who talked a lot. Joy was introverted. He reminded me of my promise.

"You have forgotten about your promise."

"What promise?"

"Remember you had told me that you would get me a green pen?"

"I will. Let me grab my purse."

I had five rupees in my purse. It was a good amount of money to buy a pen those days. He held my hand tightly while crossing the road. It gave me a sense of responsibility and happiness. As his elder sister, I loved bossing him around, but I also felt kindness I had never felt towards anyone in my life. I loved protecting him, teaching him, and pampering him. And he knew how much I loved him. Maybe that's why he never hesitated to ask me for small gifts.

Joy and I talked a lot that day. We went for a long walk. He told me about Titu, a boy who sat next to him in this class and how he had been kicking Joy while playing soccer.

"Have you told Mum about Titu?"

"No, you are the first one."

"Good. Let's not involve Mum. I will take care of this," I assured him. The last thing I wanted was to see my little brother suffer, especially after what he had been through in the residential school. I wanted to beat the crap out of Titu.

Next day, as we got down from the school bus, I gave Joy a hug and told him I was going to talk to that kid in his class. He was relieved.

We didn't have any lunchroom in our school, so we had the option to go outside and eat lunch. A lot of kids in my class preferred eating their lunch on the back lawn of the school. There were some big banyan trees. Many kids liked sitting in its shade, chatting, and eating their meals.

It was during one of those days I spotted Joy's class playing in the field. I couldn't see Joy. I ran looking for him. When I went to the field, I saw his whole class was playing soccer, except him. He was sitting in one corner quietly.

"Joy, what's the matter? Are you okay? Everyone else is playing. Why are you sitting alone?"

"I am not allowed to play with them."

"Why not?"

"Because Titu is the captain and he does not want me."

That was it. I had enough. I went straight to Titu and said, "If you ever exclude Joy again, I will throw you over that school wall."

Needless to say, Joy was included in everything, not just in soccer. But the hilarious part was that Titu and Joy became best friends a couple of months later. Joy started looking forward to going to school. And the funniest part was that when Titu came over to our house to play, his first question was, "Is your sister home?"

We still laugh about it.

Hindi Again

Even though I loved going to school and spending time studying and meeting friends, I had a secret nobody knew. I had zero confidence. My wounds were fresh and they hurt as I struggled to cope with the outer world. Most days, I cried in the bathroom. That was my only way of relieving stress.

One afternoon, I cried a little too much. My eyes were swollen and red. I didn't want anyone to see me but to my luck, my Hindi teacher, Mr. Gupta, saw me. He knew something was wrong.

"What's wrong?"

"Nothing, sir."

"Come and meet me in my class."

"Okay, coming."

My experiences with Mr. Sharma in Rampur made me cautious about the new teacher in the same subject. But I knew I would be in trouble if I didn't go, so I went.

"Come inside, please," he said rather bluntly.

I was startled by his loud voice. "Yes, sir," I murmured.

"I loved how you did the analysis of some of the short stories written by Mahadevi Verma," he complimented me.

I was pleasantly surprised.

"I tried. I am not very good in that subject," I said nervously

"Non-sense. I see a lot of potential in you. You see, Hindi is a very different language. You have to learn both the genders well," he waited for a couple of seconds, took off his huge glasses, rubbed his eyes, and continued, "I will give you a book. I use it all the time. See how the genders are assigned. It has some good translation from English words to Hindi words. You will like it."

"Thank you, sir," I said quietly as he handed me the book.

Just when I was about to step out of the room, he called me again and said, "You have seven days to memorize them all. I will take a test you after a week."

I had that book with me twenty-four hours for the next seven days. When I slept, it was below my pillow. I read it on the school bus, while eating my meals, before going to bed, and the first thing after waking up in the morning. That's the thing about encouraging and kind words. They always leave a lasting impression.

I scored nine out of ten in the test. The fact that Mr. Gupta took interest and saw my potential made me so proud. Minu was the best student in Hindi. Her first language was Hindi, and she spoke it at home while I did not. I was most comfortable in English.

"Minu, talk to Lisa only in Hindi. Work with her on the gender thing. Think of you both as a team," Mr. Gupta instructed Minu at the end of class. That helped me immensely. He also asked me to read poems and phrases from the chapter books almost every day. Initially, it was challenging and also embarrassing. My pronunciation was bad and I made a lot of mistakes. Of course, there were kids who giggled in the class. Honestly, I have to admit as time passed, I started looking forward to it. That's when I developed my interest for Hindi poems, something that I had thought all my life wasn't my cup of tea.

I worked hard in that subject. I had to prove it to myself that I could master it. And truth shone through. That's exactly what I needed for self-confidence.

Every once in a while, I stopped by to see how Joy was doing in his class and was happy to see that he was doing well.

"Why do you come to my classroom? I don't like it when you talk to my friends and my teacher," he often told me. I loved his sweet facial expressions.

"I do that because I am your sister. You are too young to tell me what to do and what not to do. I do that because I love you and I want you to do very well in school. Understood?" I responded.

Meanwhile, Mum had taken a role in the family that was unimaginable. Most days, she was exhausted after work and slept like a log. But she took great care of us. She was frugal and saved every penny.

Mum deliberately walked home from school many evenings. That was her way of saving money by not using public transport. Walking home also gave her solace and exercise. I knew she liked it.

We never went out to eat, and I had only a couple of good dresses. Mum had only five sarees, all given to her by Aunt Renu. Mum wore them, washed them, and wore them again. She never got tired of arguing about the price of the vegetables and fruits with the vendors. It was hilarious.

I accompanied Mum every once in a while, and helped her carry the grocery bags. I loved watching her bargain for the prices of the vegetables, just for the sheer joy of watching. Mum did it for all items; clothes, food, shoes, anything and everything that could be purchased.

But what was astounding was the fact that Mum wasn't bitter about her life.

One day I asked her, "Do you remember our days in Rampur, Maa? I feel upset when I think about those painful days."

Mum said, "That's what human life is. We go through a range of experiences, each so different, so unique. Tears, joys, rejections, affection, cries, and our little triumphs."

Even though Mum complained about money once in a while, deep inside she considered herself rich. I grew up in abundance. Abundance of unconditional love, tons of warmth, and unending best wishes. My grandparents and Mum were always there for me. Always.

Mum had never been very good at expressing her feelings, but now that she was happy, she decided to try. Every now and then, she gave me a hug. I treasured them. For me, those hugs carried a thousand messages of love, the light of twinkling stars, a glimpse of her love, and her toughness, greatest stories of Inspiration, and countless blessings.

. Every morning, I looked at myself in the mirror and practiced standing up for myself and voicing my opinions. I had a deep desire to master the skill of talking and not being scared to death.

Sometimes, I felt I was walking a thin line between bravery and anxiety. Some days, I was really brave to sit with Mum and tell her nice things and pep ourselves up because I knew we were all recuperating in our own ways.

But some days, I grew anxious about my future and got caught in a strange whirlwind of thoughts, *What was I going to do in life? What if I failed in my endeavors? What if I didn't have the strength to fight back? What if nothing worked out for me?*

The evenings were especially hard when I spent a lot of my free time thinking about my life's uncertainties. Being desperate was a blessing in disguise because I didn't have many options but to work.

Meanwhile when Sona stayed with us, nobody came looking for her. I know that made her sad. She never said anything to me, but she cried behind closed doors. She stayed with us for ten days and then went back to her parents' house on her own. Next day, when she came to work in the evening, she was quiet.

"Is everything okay? What did your parents say?" I asked her.

"Nothing. They don't talk to me unless it is about money."

I had a lot of homework that evening and didn't prod her more. Time flew and days passed, Sona came every evening to work without fail, but she had become quieter.

One evening as I was eating dinner, she sat by my side and said, "I left him."

"Who?"

"Raj, my boyfriend."

"Good for you, Sona. He was no good. I am proud of you," I said as I gave her a pat on the shoulder.

After a few weeks, she started to come to work irregularly. If she came for two days, then she skipped the third day. She came for few days and then skipped a couple of days. That was nothing like her.

Mum thought Sona needed time to sort things out in her life. Eventually, one day she stopped coming to work. It was a shock because she hadn't informed us about it, and we had no inkling.

Next day, while coming back from school, I stopped by at her parents' house. They told me Sona didn't live in Sambalpur anymore and she was now married off. I looked at them with a blank face, but her mother assured me that Sona was happy. I had more questions to ask, but they didn't seem interested as they were busy in their drinking session and I had sort of interrupted them.

It was a long walk for me from Sona's house that evening. I didn't believe any of the crap her parents said. I was so worried about her that I cried all the way. I refused to eat anything that night and didn't come out of my room until it was time for me to go to school the next day.

Life wasn't the same after Sona left. I longed to hear her sweet voice. She liked humming while cooking and that brought light in our mundane lives. I missed that the most. I missed her sweet smile, her generous heart, her authenticity, and her honesty.

One evening, Mum said, "Let's watch a movie together."

"No, I don't feel like watching."

"Why not?"

"Because television reminds me of Sona. I remember how she waited for me to finish homework and we watched those comedy shows before going to bed. I miss her so much, Maa."

"I know. It was fun for you girls to roll on the floor with laughter."

"I miss all that, Maa. Where did she go? She didn't tell me anything."

"We all have our plates full, Lismun. We can't think of anyone else now. The problem is that you get attached to other people way too soon. We can't solve all problems."

And Mum wasn't completely wrong. I needed to focus on myself, but it was hard, quite hard.

A couple of months later, we had some guest, and Mum sent me to the vegetable market to get some fresh tomatoes, beans, and fish.

That was where I saw Sona. I couldn't believe my eyes when I saw her. She was glowing with happiness and was wearing some beautiful silver jewelry. She came and hugged me.

"Where are you these days? Tell me about yourself. Do you know I was worried like hell?" I said in a disappointed voice.

She hugged me tighter and tears rolled down her cheeks.

"Sona, you have to talk to me. Look at me. You have let me down big time."

"I am doing real good, you know. I am married now. I am happy," she said, looking at me and then looking at the skies, as if God granted her what she wanted.

"You had a boyfriend and I was happy when you left him because he wasn't nice to you. Now you are married. I don't know what to say."

"Please don't tell me that you married the same guy."

"No, a different guy," she said with a blush on her face.

"I don't care. I wanted you to be okay. Why do you take wrong decisions for yourself?"

"I am more than okay, I am happy. Do I look sad from any angle?"

I looked at her from head to toe, scrutinizing her. She did look happy to me.

"So how did you meet this guy?" I was dying to know what happened to her in the last few months.

"Oh, it was an arranged marriage. My aunt sent the proposal for me and my parents wanted me to meet the guy. I met him once and he liked me. I liked him, too. He was different, real sweet, and real kind. The thing is that my parents wanted me out of the house."

"Why did your parents want you out of the house? You were the bread earner."

"Well, in our community, sometimes, things work differently. The groom pays the bride's family. The opposite of dowry actually."

"Sona, I like plain, simple, and sweet things. What you are saying is too complicated for me. I can't understand it. Explain it to me, please."

"My parents married me off to this guy and took a lot of money from him."

She paused for a minute while I waited with my eyes open and my jaw was about to drop. Then she continued, "But I got lucky. My husband is a nice man. Finally, I am happy. I am at peace. I have my own home now. He takes care of me. Some days, he even cooks for me. He does not want me to work. And you know what, I have started reading books now. One step at a time, I will finish the tenth-grade board exam someday."

Once she said that, I let go of all my anger and was so happy.

"Yay!" I screamed with joy.

It was in the middle of the vegetable market and it sounded odd. A passerby asked me if I needed help because I was too loud. And that was the last time I saw Sona. She was happy and content.

That night, when we were done with dinner, I told Mum, "I met Sona, and you know she is married now."

"Really?" Mum was, too, surprised.

"Yes, not to her boyfriend. Her parents found a nice groom for her. You know, Maa, he keeps her happy. She is even contemplating going back to school."

"Oh, that's so nice," Mum said while folding the laundry piled on the sofa.

"But how can that happen? She had an arranged marriage."

Mum laughed out aloud and said, "And who told you that arranged marriages are not good all the time. Your grandparents had an arranged marriage and that foundation is rock solid."

I had a smile on my face when I went to bed that night.

When Mum kissed me good night, she said smilingly, "I am happy for Sona. But now I have to do all the work in the house with no help."

We both laughed and I drifted to sleep soon.

Mr. Pal

On a rainy morning during the school assembly, I recited 'The Charge of the Light Brigade' by Alfred Tennyson.

"You like poems?" said someone.

"Yes, sir. I do," I said. I used the word *sir* because he definitely looked like a teacher.

"Okay, good. I am your English teacher for the next three years."

That's how I met, my favorite teacher, Mr. Pal. He was an absolute favorite among all the students, not just me. As I spent more time in his classroom, I realized he truly was a magician. He could easily convert an hour of learning to pure happiness. He had anecdotes for every chapter he read to us. He was a great story teller and knew how to spin and weave the ideas and put them in words. A teacher par excellence! Yet, he was so grounded. The best lesson he taught us was the ability to converse. He taught us that words were omnipotent. One reckless word could cause havoc. One sweet word could melt a glacier.

He could influence people with just a few words and expressions, sometimes even with silence. We thrived under his guidance. Sometimes, he would ask us to write an essay on a particular topic while he stepped out of the classroom. Even in his absence, he could influence each one of us. A lot of students, who sat in the last benches in the classroom, didn't do well in other subjects. But they did well in English.

To me, personally, I think he was God sent. He took me under his wings. I never had a teacher in my life who had influenced me so much. He spoke less and understood more. He hated less and loved more. He preached less and modeled more.

In one of my first classes with him, when Mr. Pal asked me a question related to some analysis I had done, my eyes were focused on the ground.

"Look up and make eye contact when you talk."

"But we are told to bow down when we talk to elders."

"Who tells you that?"

"I guess, society," I said hesitantly because I didn't know the right answer.

"Then don't listen to the society. If it teaches you the wrong thing and conveys the incorrect message for life, then say bye, bye to such rules and regulations."

When we did our school play that year, Mr. Pal wrote and directed it. It was about a queen, and he let me write the opening lines.

This is what I wrote,

'The bluish, green water of the vast ocean takes her life for a ride with it. With the ups and downs of the waves, she experienced excitement, fear, anxiety, ecstasy, curiosity but most of all, love that touched her in the ocean, above and beyond it.'

Chapter Sixteen

Gossips

It was a cold night in the month of December. Mum had to attend a teachers' conference in a nearby town next day. She had an early morning train to catch. So, the night before, Mum prepared dinner early.

Food was warm and was on the dining table when Joy and I came back after playing badminton. Mum was about to do some knitting when the we walked inside the house.

"Dinner is on the table. Wash your hands before we eat. We got to go to bed early tonight," Mum said lovingly.

Mum's second cousin, Mita Aunty, knocked at the front door and I opened it.

"Oh, Hello Aunty. How are you? Have a seat. I will call Maa," I said as I walked her inside the living room.

I didn't hate Mita Aunty, but I didn't like her either. Some days, she was extremely nice and friendly; some days, she was bitter and sarcastic. As I went inside to call Mum, I wondered what was her mood that day.

"Nina, how are you, my dear?" she asked Mum.

"I am doing good."

"I am here to talk about something... Hmmmm...something very important."

"Really? What's that? Well, let me make tea for you while you tell me the important thing," Mum said while walking towards the stove to make tea.

"Mum, please make tea for me, too. I will go change my clothes later," I said while untying my shoelaces.

In our house, we all loved tea with tea power, whole milk, and lots of sugar. I drank three-four cups a day.

"It would be nice if we talk in the absence of your kids. I mean if you politely ask Lisa to go from here," Mita Aunty said in a whispering tone and gesturing towards me.

Mum didn't like it and her face showed it. I was determined not to go because I wanted to know what she had in her mind. So, I stayed there, and my eyes focused on her now.

"It's okay. You can talk in front of Lisa," Mum said, while looking at the boiling water and milk on the stove.

"Are you never going back to your husband?" she asked Mum.

Mum looked at her in complete disbelief but maintained her composure and said, "I am really busy these days. My job as an elementary school teacher, two kids, this big house, parents. I have a lot on my plate. I can't think of anything else."

But even then, Mita Aunty didn't stop and continued shamelessly, "No, I mean, seriously, how will you lead your life without your husband? There is a cruel world out there. It will be very difficult for you."

Mum smiled and said, "Don't worry about me. I will be fine."

The ease with which Mum spoke made Mita Aunty very uncomfortable. She was about to say something when my grandparents returned from their routine evening walk. Mum thought that was a good opportunity for the question answer session with her cousin, so she said, "Mom, Dad, look who is here. I have made tea for all of you. Come and talk to Mita."

My grandparents spent the rest of the evening with Mita Aunty while Mum and I went to bed.

The next day, I woke up at four in the morning with Mum. As Mum got ready to go for her conference, I made tea and cucumber sandwich for breakfast.

As we were sipping tea, I asked Mum, "Why do people want to know so much about us?"

"Because this is India and people around us are curious."

"That's called gossip, Maa," I said in an angry voice.

"I have made myself unpopular by walking out of my marriage."

"That is hilarious because it is your life and it does not concern them."

"I know. But there are some people who love to talk, people who give you unsolicited advice. You can't do anything about them. Don't worry, Lismun."

It made me sick when I pondered how people thrived on their curiosity to know about other people. Most people never spoke a word to her face, maybe that's why it hadn't bothered me so far. But with Mum's cousin asking direct questions like that, I was little disturbed. I couldn't let it go. It just bothered me that people were nosy. Nobody knew the real story except me, Mum, and Joy.

"Why do people feel entitled to know about others when they can't help?" I asked Mum again.

"Sometimes, you have to let go of things. You don't owe any explanation to anybody. Mum said while putting oil on my hair."

"You have to take care of your hair. It looks frizzled. Don't forget to put oil on your hair before going to bed. You are a big girl now, Lismun. I can't take care of you forever."

"Why are you so concerned about my hair?" I asked Mum.

"Yes, that one you got is right. I don't care about what people think and do but I am concerned about your hair, because it does not look very good right now."

Mum left for her conference an hour later and I sat there thinking about how Mum put her priorities in life.

My frizzled hair was a bigger concern for Mum than the gossips. I learned that day that Mita Aunty wasn't the first or the last pea brained idiot with a big mouth I was going to meet in my life. Gossipmongers often flocked together. Just like gossips were transient, so would be the gossipmongers and it was not worth my time or Mum's time.

Another try

Life had become peaceful for me, Mum, and Joy. I had settled down in a daily routine, and I liked it that way. My father never called us, not even to talk to Joy.

But one time, he sent us a telegram and asked us to meet him at a cafeteria. Mum decided not to go. Another time he sent his friend to our house with his wife and kids, uninvited. The friend tried convincing Mum to go back to my father. Mum smiled and asked them to stay for dinner and then politely declined. I actually found it hilarious.

But I wondered why my father never came himself. He tried one last time by sending his brother. Uncle Tola had always been okay to us and had never told us anything hurtful. I wasn't close to his family, but I sort of liked them. Mum was the same, I guess. So, my uncle stopped by one weekend. It was almost lunch time and we were getting ready to eat. He was accompanied by his wife and two little daughters.

"Go and get some fish from the vegetable market," Mum said to me.

"Why do you always send me to get things for you when we have guests?" I said.

"Because you are my sweet daughter and I have nobody else. Go, please," Mum coaxed me a little more. So, I went grudgingly.

When I returned, Mum had already made rice and curry. She made some yummy fish fry in pure coconut oil and we all had a great lunch.

My uncle's two little girls were affectionate and talkative. I was still trying to figure out why they had come. Finally, when we all sat down to have coffee after eating lunch, he broached the topic. "I think my brother really wants you all in his life. He is repentant. Will you please consider going back to him with the kids?" he said softly.

"We are fine. It's not about him anymore. It's about the kids," Mum was polite as usual but stood her ground.

"See, I know you are mad at him. But think about it. How are you ever going to bring up these two kids all by yourself? You will surely need him at some point."

I listened quietly to what he said. I was nervous and a little scared. I didn't know what the outcome was going to be. At that time, my greatest fear was of Mum succumbing to the pressure and taking us back to my father. It had taken fifteen years for Mum to walk out of all the trauma and abuse. The last thing I wanted was to go through all that again.

As my thoughts were tossing and turning inside my head, I heard Mum talk.

"No, we are good here. I don't want to go back. The kids don't want to go back. We are fine here. We will manage. Please go and tell your brother that we are not coming back," Mum said firmly.

My uncle was losing patience by now, so he stood up to leave. His wife, who was sipping coffee, held the half empty cup in an awkward way and tried to finish it as fast as she could. He gestured her to stand and she did so hurriedly. She spilled the rest of the coffee on her saree as she stood up. Mum got a towel for her.

"Here, clean yourself well," Mum said to her affectionately.

My uncle tried convincing Mum one more time, "When the kids apply to colleges and all that, you will need their father's signature. This is going to be a real problem. Think about it."

"I am so happy that you and your family think about us. I am so grateful. The main reason I am here at my father's house with both my kids, with a meagre amount of money is because I want my kids to go to college and mind their own lives. As far as the signatures on the papers and documents are concerned, I think it will be okay. Don't think so much about us. We will be fine," Mum said assertively and in the coolest way possible.

I never forgot how Mum talked that afternoon. I couldn't figure out whether it was heart felt or sarcastic.

For obvious reasons, my uncle didn't look very thrilled about it. He held his daughters' hands and instructed his wife to walk out of the door.

Mum was tired after cooking and cleaning, so she went to take an afternoon *siesta*. I stood near the window and watched my uncle and his family leave. His toddler daughter waved goodbye to me and flashed a sweet smile. I waved at her and very soon, they disappeared out of my sight.

Out of all my relatives from my father's side, I liked this uncle and his wife because, unlike others, they were always civil. Deep down, Maa liked his wife, too. But strangely, I felt relieved that day and was thankful for the decision Mum made. I just wanted to be alone. Maybe I was tired, too.

That evening when Mum prepared tea for me. I watched her closely. She boiled the water, then mixed the milk, and put the tea powder in it. She let it boil until it became orangish brown.

"You okay, Maa?" I asked her.

"Oh, yes. I am just fine."

"Looks like you are thinking about something," I asked her again.

"Just looking at the color of chai. It looks good. I am sure it will taste great, too," she said quietly.

Grandpa Met Mr. Pal

Mr. Pal had no idea about my family situation. When the report cards were sent home for that semester, he sent mine with my father's name on it. Grandpa signed it and brought it back to school. I stood near the door as they spoke to each other.

"Thank you, Mr. Mahapatra. So nice to meet you. I have never met Lisa's parents and I would love to meet them someday."

Grandpa explained the whole situation to Mr. Pal.

"So, Lisa's father has no interest in being in her life? She is such a sweet girl," Mr. Pal said.

"Unfortunately, that is how it is. You can always call me or my daughter about Lisa."

"I know even when parents get separated, the fathers always remain a big part of their kids' lives."

"He says he wants the whole family back, but my daughter does not want to go back. He hasn't come and talked to us at all about his kids. I don't know what future holds for these kids. My job as a grandpa is to love them unconditionally and that is what I am doing. These two kids have been through a lot and I don't think they will ever heal, but I will try my best."

"We don't get to choose everything in life. Do we Mr. Mahapatra?" Mr. Pal said.

"No, we certainly don't."

"Lisa seems to be doing very well. I had no idea about her family situation," Mr. Pal opened the windows to get some fresh air.

As Grandpa and I rode our bikes home that evening, I felt weird that my life story could make someone sad. But that's the truth, it did. I hoped to become thick-skinned someday and rise above the pain hidden in my eyes and heart.

That night, I wrote before going to bed,

'No matter what, when life sings a melodious song, sing along with it. Learn the lyrics. Learn the music. Sing it to yourself, uplift your spirits when you are surrounded by chaos. Our loved ones, our good memories, the affection that we receive from others, our little triumphs; they are all part of the melodious song.'

Chapter Seventeen

March 1993, Sambalpur, India

Winter was almost over and it was the month of March. All tenth graders had to write the very important board exam. On the first day of the exam, I was well prepared, and I knew I was going to ace it. As I walked out of the house to go to school, Mum gave me a kiss and a tight hug. I smiled and waved at Grandpa. He was watching me from the family room window. I took my bike out and rode it fast and pretty soon, I disappeared in the busy crowd on the road.

After my exams were over, I had more time to do things that I liked. Summer vacation was fun. One of the luxuries I enjoyed during hot summer days was eating mangoes. Grandpa loved them too and went to the local market every morning to get mangoes. Sometimes, he got four-five different varieties.

Even though I was having so much fun, deep inside, I worried about my results. I had done well in my board exams and I couldn't wait to see what rank I was going to get in my class that year.

It gave me a lot of time to read and write. Aunt Renu, Uncle Himansu and Litun visited us for three weeks during that summer vacation.

Uncle Himansu taught English to university students and he was reading Vikram Seth's "A Suitable Boy" those days. It was a big book with more than fourteen hundred pages. When he left, he gave me the book to read. I got so engrossed that I read that book day in and day out until I finished it. It contained many political and social facets behind the family drama.

It was little hard for me to keep track with all the characters and relationships but by the time I finished it, I had learned a lot. I wrote a beautiful book review in a local magazine. To me, that was time well spent. It was an achievement in itself.

Our tenth board results were out in June. I had the highest total score. What I was most proud of was my score in Hindi. I had the second highest score in the class after Minu, just one mark less than hers.

That gave me a feeling that anything and everything was within my reach. I came home and wrote down my long-term goals that included a goal of writing engineering entrances after my senior year.

Junior year

That was the best year of school for me, my grades were fantastic and I made tons of friends. I followed a routine at home, all thanks to Grandpa. I could squeeze in everything in my schedule.

I loved reading Shakespeare and Charles Dickens the most. That year was the time when I built my foundation of writing. I bought a new green diary from the local market and wrote in it every single day. When I wrote, I felt I was talking. As time passed, I became more expressive, as if my thoughts were my words.

To me, words could melt my heart, pierce through my soul, and cut my heart into a thousand pieces. The words I wrote brightened my day but could also dampen my spirits, so I tried focusing only on the positives.

I told Grandpa, "Words are amazing, Grandpa, aren't they?"

"What do I know about words? You are the scholar," he said with a smile on his face.

"You don't have to be scholar to understand words. You know, I have started to think that words and songs are the most powerful media in the world. Songs because they have music and words. Grandpa, do you know about the huge ship Titanic?"

"Yes, I do."

"When it was about to sink, do you know what some people did?"

"What?"

"They sang. When the giant ship was about to sink, a lot of people knew they were going to die, so some people started to sing. It was frigid, and the ship was sinking fast, yet they continued singing. They sang to calm themselves, but in the process, they managed to uplift other despondent souls. Suddenly, death wasn't the most intimidating thing and more people started singing. The united voice became louder."

"Good to know that, Lisa," Grandpa said.

Chapter Eighteen

Shanti

Some friends enter in our lives to remain forever. They touch our lives at so many different levels and in beautiful ways. That's how Shanti was. Her parents were from the north of India but had settled down in Sambalpur in eastern India. She was the eldest of the four girls. Her father was a school teacher. He taught Hindi in an elementary school in Sambalpur.

In many ways, we were quite similar. Her parents expected good behavior and had high expectations from her, just the way Mum had from me. With Shanti as my best friend, my life was different. We shared the sweetness of dreams and fragrance of hopes. When we talked, we didn't judge each other. When we cried, we didn't push each other away and when we were silent, we didn't ignore each other.

I cherished her presence in my life and she felt the same about me. The foundation of our friendship was based on mutual admiration. We respected each other and valued each other's opinions. She knew what I was thinking and finished my sentences for me. She stood by me when I was wrong and she supported me when I was right. And I did the same.

I had a side of me that was naughty. My friend, Annie, lived in a small university town near Sambalpur. She got the tastiest food in her lunch every day. One day, two of the girls in my class came up with the master idea of skipping class for the whole day and going to her house to eat.

When they looked at me, I smiled and said, "Let's do it."

So, the next morning after school assembly, we traveled to her house in the local bus. We had a feast at Annie house that day; fried rice, lamb curry, chutney, rice crispy, noodles, and lots of sweet treats.

When we returned to the school, it was almost three in the afternoon and we had missed most of the classes. To enter the school campus, we had to climb up the wall. I was the first one to do it.

Just when I jumped inside, I saw Mr. Pal standing there.

"We had a good class today, didn't we?" he asked me in a sarcastic tone.

"Sorry, sir," I could barely speak.

"Look up. I have told you many times, when you talk, you need to look up."

"Yes," I said, the guilt inside me was making it hard to make eye contact with him.

"Go inside your class and grab your bag. It's time to go home."

Each of the girls followed me one after another.

We went back home after thirty minutes or so.

I confided in Grandpa that night about what had happened.

"I committed a blunder."

"And what is that blunder?"

"I skipped school today to go to Annie's house and just hang out."

"You did? Alone?"

"No, all the girls in the class."

"Okay, so what's the blunder?"

"I mean skipping classes for the whole day."

"It's okay. This is life, my dear. You need to experience everything. You need to fall to learn to walk."

Next morning, I dreaded entering the classroom, but did anyway.

"You aren't planning on skipping the class today, are you?" Mr. Pal asked.

"No, sir."

"That's good. You can only skip one day of class in four years and your quota is over," he smiled. It made my heart feel so light and I never repeated that mistake.

Junior and Senior Years

My junior and senior years in high school taught me a lot about friendship, tolerance, and love. Our house in Sambalpur was below ground level and was close to a river. When it rained, that area was often flooded.

In 1994, during the monsoon season, the rain didn't stop for nearly three days and there was water on the first floor of the house. Fortunately, we lived on the second floor and it didn't affect us much. But the roads were closed, and life came to stand still. I had missed a couple of days of school because it was almost impossible to walk outside.

Eventually when the rain subsided and the water level went down, Grandpa said, "I think you should go to school today. Finally, the unceasing rain has stopped. The roads are looking good and the bus should be able to pick up the kids from this side of town."

He was right. School bus did come that morning to pick us up. But there was muddy water in front of the house. Grandpa held our polished shoes, clean socks, and two towels. He asked Joy and me to walk up to the bus stop in bare feet. Once we crossed the muddy patch, we cleaned our feet with the towels, and he gave us our shoes to wear.

When I went inside the bus and waved at Grandpa, he smiled back and waved at me holding those dirty towels on his shoulders. He was someone who had touched me so deeply that mere words were inadequate to express how I felt. I knew that moment that I would carry the flame of his kindness forever in my heart.

After a couple of months, my grandparents renovated the first floor of the house. We got a sweet family as a tenant once the work was over. I loved them and they were affectionate towards me. The only problem was that they had a new-born baby daughter and she cried all the time.

I told Mum, "What's up with these little babies? Why do they cry so much?"

Mum laughed loudly, "Lismun, because babies are babies and they can't talk. They express everything by crying."

"I don't know all that. I just feel all babies are bald headed, pink faced imbeciles."

Mum was shocked to hear that. She became annoyed.

"What's wrong with you, Lismun? How can you not like babies?"

"I like babies, Maa, but I just don't like their constant crying."

"I can't believe the way you talk sometimes. What's wrong with you?"

Mum stormed out of my room. And I followed her.

"Why are you following me, Lisa?" Mum reprimanded me.

"Because I didn't like how you walked out of the door now, Maa."

"Lisa, you are scaring me off. How can you talk like that? Seriously, you don't like babies? What type of mother you will become?"

"Maa, take it slow. What makes you think that I will get married and I will even have kids. For God's sake, slow down. I haven't even finished high school yet."

"What? You may not get married?"

"I don't know, Maa. I have a lot of time to think about all that."

I thought making Mum understand was futile, so I left things as they were.

After a few weeks, I told Grandpa, "I will be writing tons of engineering entrance examinations."

"That's nice, Lisa,"

"Grandpa, I want to let you know that I may not be in Sambalpur when I join engineering."

"That's fine. It is your life and you can go anywhere you want."

It was around that time Grandpa started teaching a lot of neighborhood kids during afternoons.

"Why are you teaching these kids, Grandpa?" I was so curious to know what he really thought.

"Because they have nobody to teach them."

"So, does it mean that you will teach everyone in this world? You need to take care of your health. Why are you straining yourself?"

"There is no problem. I can teach them for a couple of hours in the afternoon, Lisa."

I couldn't figure out why he wanted to work so hard after retirement. After some weeks, I stood behind him as he taught the kids spellings. He was involved and he looked happy, genuinely happy. The kids thrived at school and were grateful for the help they received from Grandpa.

I wasn't sure but I guessed that Grandpa knew he was going to miss me after I moved out of the house, so he found a way to engage himself.

During my junior year in high school, I enrolled myself in physics tutoring classes. Shanti and I went for the classes together.

One day, when we came outside after the classes were over, it was raining cats and dogs. Shanti's father stood under a tree with his bicycle and on the side, I saw Grandpa waiting for me, totally drenched, holding an umbrella for me.

Next morning, when we were eating lunch, Shanti said, "The ground beneath our feet is so swampy."

"I know," I said.

"But we can push ourselves out of this."

"Yes, we can."

And we did. The eighteen months or so went by fast. Shanti stayed at our place some nights to study. It was fun. When we got tired, we cooked noodles at four in the morning.

Uncle Bhanja came to live with us for few months around that time. He wasn't doing well, had lost weight, and often talked about winning the fields medal for mathematics.

"But I think it is given to people below forty, uncle," I reminded him.

"They will make an exception for me," he said.

I knew something was wrong with Uncle Bhanja because what he talked didn't make sense. He often sat alone and talked to himself. It made Grandpa sad, but he kept himself busy and taught more students. I got busier with my exams while Mum was busy running the house single-handedly. Grandma had sort of become a recluse and spent a lot of time praying God.

The Beginning of My Undergraduate Days, Bhubaneswar, 1996

Finally, when my engineering results were out, I decided to move to Bhubaneswar to study Electronics and Telecommunications Engineering.

As I prepared to go to the dorm, I was excited. I thought living away from home would be a new experience. I knew I was going to miss Mum and Grandpa. But I was very excited, all I wanted was to make new friends and be independent. The thought of dorm life fascinated me.

One evening, I sat down with Mum and Grandpa as they were making a monthly budget for my course.

"Who is going to drop me in Bhubaneswar?" I asked.

"I can go. Maybe Joy will come with us, too," Mum said.

"But that way Joy will miss school. I don't want that, Maa."

"I will go with Lisa," Grandpa said.

"I think that will be good," I said with a happy face.

Two weeks later, we took an early morning bus from Sambalpur to Bhubaneswar. It took us nearly eight hours. When we reached there, we were starving.

"Let's find a restaurant where we can eat fish curry and rice, Grandpa," I said.

And we found one. It was one of the best meals of my life, maybe because we were so hungry. Hot rice, delicious fish curry, and a glass of mango *lassi* were heaven.

After a heavy lunch, we went shopping. We bought comforters, bedsheets, pillows, a blue table lamp, slippers, plates, spoons, forks, and a dozen of water bottles. That evening, Grandpa dropped me in my dorm, what we called hostel in India.

"This is your home for the next four years. I will write to you regularly. You take care of yourself, my dear," he said.

"I can't believe I have to live without you, grandma and Mum. How am I going to survive?"

He wiped my tears and said, "People who love you live with you no matter where you are, Lisa."

Grandpa took an overnight bus that night to come back to Sambalpur. After he left, I went to bed straight. Unfortunately, my undergraduate days weren't what I had planned for and they turned out to be challenging. I didn't fit in. My course work was okay, but I liked nothing about the ambience or place. I didn't like the food, my room, and the city. My being severely homesick didn't help either.

I knew I wasn't a cool kid, yet I had no desire to change myself. I read and wrote during my free time. When I was in a party or gathering, I didn't know what to talk and I couldn't relate to anything other students talked about.

I was weird. I was stick thin and talked fast. Most of the time, my hair was uneven because I cut my own hair. I wore big glasses, which were totally out of fashion. In reality, for me to be different was actually a matter of conviction.

Following the traditional road did not do any good to me and I stuck with my own style. At that point of time, if there was an award for the greatest weirdo in the world, without an iota of doubt, I would have been the winner.

The boys outnumbered the girls in the engineering college. I loved participating in debates but there weren't many girls there. I had no qualm about standing among boys and talking about history or Indian politics.

I wore baggy jeans and never used make up. I spoke what I felt. So, a lot of boys thought I was arrogant, a rebel, and a tomboy. Some girls thought I was an altogether different creature as I was nothing like them.

It wasn't my fault completely. I tried. But after a couple of months, I thought I didn't belong there and felt I was surrounded by strangers.

At the end of the day, we all want to be accepted and loved for who we are. Each one of us. People say that we are all unique, each human being is different from the other. Not true. There is something common between all of us and I am not talking about the basic need of food, shelter, and clothes. I am talking about a wish, a desire, a motto, and a dream. We all want to be loved, accepted, and valued. You take any two human beings, totally different, with complete opposite facets of personalities; this one trait is common. Their need to be loved is universal. I was not an exception to that and deep inside, I wanted to make some good friends.

A girl, who lived in another dorm, suggested to change the type of clothes I wore. Most of the clothes I had were stitched by Mum, maybe that's why I made a hard choice. I decided that night that I was going to stick to what I was and wasn't going to change myself for anybody.

My room was huge, and we also had a balcony attached to it. I felt so lonely at times that I cried for hours. The balcony was a big relief for me. I sat there crying many evenings. Sometimes I didn't know what made me cry.

To my relief, I bonded well with some of the seniors. One of them was a voracious reader and she invited me to her room to talk about books.

But deep inside, I had built a cocoon around myself. I was happy and comfortable in there. It made me feel safe.

The kitchen was on the first floor of the building. There was a cook who cooked for all the girls. We didn't have a common dining room. So, every night, we brought our dinner to the room to eat. It had become the norm and I guess we liked it that way.

One evening, when we all came back from our respective classes, I had high fever. I couldn't take my asthma medicines without eating food. I was too weak to go downstairs to get dinner. I slept off that evening and didn't feel like eating dinner.

I walked down and it was getting dark. I walked for half a mile to make a phone call to Mum from a local booth.

"Hi, Maa," I said.

"Hey, sweetie. How are you?" Mum asked me.

"I want to come home."

"Why? You have your exams now. Don't you?"

"Yes."

"What's going on?"

"I feel lonely."

And I hung up the phone. When I came back, I was starving. But the kitchen was closed, so I went to bed hungry that night.

Next day, I took a fever reducer tablet and went for circuit theory classes. When I came back, Mum was waiting for me in the lobby.

"You are here, Maa," I held her tightly and broke down.

Mum stayed with me for a few days until I finished my exams, but she had to leave because she had her job and had left Joy with my grandparents.

A week later, I was sick again. The new semester was yet to begin, and I had a break for a few days. Next day, I dragged myself out of the bed, and called Aunt Renu. By that afternoon, I was in the bus to Berhampur, where she worked. It was four hours bus ride from Bhubaneswar, and I have no idea how I traveled in that condition. But I made it. They took me to a doctor right away and it turned out that I had a severe respiratory infection. I stayed at my aunt's place for ten days. She really took great care of me. She gave me some pocket money and bought some beautiful dresses for me.

When I recuperated and felt good to come back to the dorm, I came back to Bhubaneswar. I was grateful for what Aunt Renu did for me. I took two days off and rested in the dorm. When I recovered completely, I went back to school.

I took my old dairy from high school days to the hostel. I wrote every single week, every Friday night, to be precise. One Saturday morning, I woke up and found my diary missing. Most of the time, it was either on my table or near my pillow. I couldn't find it anywhere that morning. I grew restive as I ran around looking for it.

To my relief, I found my diary a couple of hours later on the balcony of our room. Some of the pages were torn. I really didn't know what had happened. That was a puzzle I could never solve.

I have to admit that the thing that bothered me the most in Bhubaneswar was the void I felt deep inside. My heart ached when I saw the parents of other girls, especially when their fathers came to meet them. There was a girl in my batch and her father came to meet her every month without fail. He was a sweet man and always asked me, "How are you, kiddo?"

It made me cry. I had never felt jealous of anyone in my life maybe because I thought I could get anything if I sincerely tried. But I felt jealous of her for the first time in my life.

Human relationships are unfathomable. Every time I saw someone's father in the lobby waiting for his daughter, I longed for that fatherly love that I never received. The worst thing was that I didn't know how to deal with those feelings.

Soon, we all got busy with our second semester. It was difficult for me, mostly because of my thoughts. I missed home too much. I called Mum and Grandpa every single night. Those phone calls took away a lot of my pocket money.

The day I had my last exam, I came to my room and there was nobody inside. I was exhausted. A lot of girls were out that evening because exams were over. I went to the balcony and bawled for hours, mostly because I felt completely lonely.

The intensity of my raw hurt feelings tripled as I let my ignorant mind be crowded with those detrimental thoughts. In my defense, I tried diverting my mind. But I didn't succeed.

As the fire of sadness engulfed me, I wanted to escape, but there was no door. I sat down quietly to study, but I couldn't concentrate.

I thought about my father that evening a lot. He never loved Mum, but how come he never loved his kids. I had just one question in my mind, *Why? How could my father not love me? I was a sweet, loving, and affectionate kid. Why was he always angry around us? Why had he never made an attempt to meet me all these years? Why did he never want to know about me? What had I done to deserve that? Fathers were supposed to love their daughters.*

I felt the ultimate betrayal. My heart was wounded and was bleeding profusely.

I sat there looking at the leaves of a huge mango tree that touched the terrace. It was around ten or so when a friend came to check on me for and I regained my senses.

My classes began in a week. I was miserable for the next few days and had no interest to be in Bhubaneswar. I was a total misfit there. I hated getting up in the mornings, and I hated going to bed. It was as if I had no dream, no vision in life. It sucked, because for me, life without dreams felt like death.

A month later, I decided to call it quits. I was convinced that I had tried my best. This was my limit and I decided to go back to Sambalpur. I packed my bags, my boxes, folded my clothes neatly, and bought myself a one-way bus ticket to go back to Sambalpur.

Not Ready

I reached home at four in the morning. It was still dark.

Grandpa opened the door. "Lisa, my dear. I can't believe what I am seeing here. Is it you? What a pleasant surprise!" he said in a really joyful voice.

I looked at him. He looked tired and his face had more wrinkles than ever. He had lost weight. That made me even more sad.

I didn't say anything. No words. All I needed was a hug from him, and I know he needed a hug from me, too.

"Why have you come back, Lisa? Your college is in session," he asked me.

"I don't know," I wasn't ready to talk about my deepest fear yet.

I had brought vanilla pastries from Bhubaneswar for everyone. I left the big box of sweets on my table and I went to sleep around six in the morning. I slept the whole day. When Joy and Mum came back from school that evening, we all sat down to eat.

"Wow! They are delish. Where did you get these from?" Grandpa said after eating the first bite.

"Some store in Sahid Nagar. I can't remember the name," I said, making it clear that I was in no mood to talk.

The dining room was partially dark. The windows were closed. I could see Mum's face from the rays of dim light of from the skylight above the window. She looked worried.

Out of nowhere, Mum put her hand on my back and started stroking. I felt safe and loved. At that point, I realized that the sweetest thing about love was that it made you a better person. That melted a lot of the bitterness and hurt I carried inside me. Well, not all the hurt, but a big chunk of it.

I had been home for more than a week, but I had hardly spoken to anyone about anything. I was quiet and spent all my free time sleeping or just tossing and turning on my bed. I sort of liked it that way, even though I knew that everyone was getting restive around me.

One night, Mum tried talking to me after dinner, but I refused. That night, I woke up screaming because of extreme pain in my calf muscles. Mum came and pressed my legs for a long time that night.

When I woke up in the morning, I found it hard to walk. My whole body was aching. I sat down on the rocking chair with excruciating pain. Grandma got some hot water and soaked it with water to massage my legs. Grandpa joined her after some time.

As I sat there crying with pain, my grandparents sat on the floor taking care of my aching legs and feet. Mum got me a heating pad to put on my back. My whole body was burning with fever. Suddenly, the feeling of guilt overwhelmed me. I felt bad that I was cold to the people who loved me the most. There was more to life, more to see, more to feel, and more to receive. And there I was, behaving like a brat and not talking.

"Grandpa, I want to confide in you," I started to cry.

"Yes, what is it, dear?"

"I struggle to be happy when I am away from home. I can't be at peace with myself. I miss home. I miss you the most," I said in a quivering voice.

"Remember the theory of Charles Darwin? Survival of the fittest? Well, that is what it is about. Our brain is very strange. It is wired in a way that it protects us. What would you do if you see a snake now? You would start running. What would you do if you saw a train coming towards you? You would run in a different direction. No doubt about it. So, think in that way," Grandpa said with a sweet smile

I had no idea what he was talking about. I was impatient and was in no mood to listen to his lectures, "You mean to say that my brain is telling me to miss home?"

"No, my dear," he said in an assertive tone.

I threw up on the floor and wanted to sleep because the throbbing headache was killing me.

"Are you okay, Lisa?" he asked.

"I feel very sick, Grandpa."

I spent the next ten days recovering from typhoid fever. Grandpa spent a lot of time by my bedside holding my hands. He was always there when I was awake. It amazed me how cheerful and content he was, as if he wore rose colored glasses, every second of the day.

When I recovered and started eating normal food, Grandpa and I made a quick trip to Balangir for two days. It helped to calm my troubled mind and channel my thoughts. That trip was exactly what I needed at that point of time.

Grandpa loved talking to people. Balangir was his hometown and there was always someone or the other who came and greeted him. He had the ability of being in other peoples' shoes and understand their situations.

I liked talking to people, too, as long as they didn't ask me anything about my dorm life or my engineering degree. It was a nice change for me as I saw Grandpa interact with his family members. We went to the fields to see vegetables. We ate on banana leaves, sitting on the floor. All meals were cooked fresh and there were several dishes of various fish. It was a fun trip.

When we were coming back to Sambalpur, Grandpa asked, "You have to tell me why you came back from Bhubaneswar. It has been more than three weeks now. When will you go back? You are missing all your classes."

"I don't like the college."

"You mean you didn't like your course, your professors?"

"No, those things didn't bother me. I don't like Bhubaneswar."

Grandpa laughed.

"Bhubaneswar is beautiful."

"I know."

"What's the problem then?"

"I don't like the people."

"What?"

"I always thought you are a people's person."

"Yes. I am. But I don't fit in there. People there are very different from me."

"Come on, don't say that. You are such a kind person. You will be just fine. You have a heart of gold my dear."

"I don't know, Grandpa. I feel broken."

Grandpa smiled and I got even more irritated.

"Why are you smiling, Grandpa? This is it. I can't take more than this," I told him.

"I can't believe that you came back because of that. That's it. That's all it took to break you? You let me down today."

Grandpa had never spoken to me like that and I was shocked.

"Grandpa, I am not here to let someone down or let someone up. I can't believe you are mocking me. You are my grandpa. You are supposed to love and stand by me."

"Lisa, I am not mocking you. But seriously, I had thought you were stronger than that. I thought you knew it well that our problems are smaller than us. We, as people, are supreme and our problems can never be bigger. Deep inside you know it, Lisa. You are such a resilient human being. You have come out of a tough situation and you have made the most of it. Haven't you?"

"The truth is that I can't live in Bhubaneswar."

"Why not?"

"I feel homesick."

"Okay, that part I understand. So, what do you plan to do right now?"

"I don't know. I will have to think about it."

"Do you have any other plan?"

"No, I don't."

"Then don't quit, Lisa. Quitting becomes a habit and as you age, you will not like it. Keep going. Go back to Bhubaneswar, finish your course, and don't let anything touch you. Fly up high. An eagle does not get drenched in the rain because it flies above the clouds. You become your own positive force to reckon with. Look we are all here, all of us, anytime you need us. Lisa, you are way smarter than the people who hurt you. This is your chance to fly and build your own nest. Build your nest up there, way above the clouds."

"Thank you, Grandpa. I don't know why I feel like crying all the time. Nothing interests me. I feel terrible when I am in the class and my eyes get filled up with tears for no reason. I hate being emotional. I have no good quality."

"Being emotional is not a bad quality. Absolutely not."

"I tried adjusting," I was biting my nails and crying profusely.

"I am not saying you didn't try. I know you did. But here is the truth. We are surrounded by a small version of the real world. When we try and escape from our situations and move to a new place, we think we will be okay. But truth prevails, my dear."

"See that's exactly what my problem is. I just don't know how to deal with these problems."

"I doubt if anyone knows that art perfectly. There is nothing called total happiness or a problem-free world. Every person is different and there are just two ways to deal with them. Either come up with a strategy to deal with every single personality in this world or develop blinders. Since doing the first one is nearly impossible, the second one looks doable to me."

When we reached Sambalpur, I spent a couple of days writing in my dairy and introspecting what I really wanted in life. I wrote for more than eight hours straight and kind of put my whole life story on the paper. Surprisingly, it made things quite clear for me and I could see the whole picture with so much of transparency. It dawned on me that I was the glue, I was the strength, and I was the string that kept all of us going. I wasn't going to be sucked in a black hole of misery, helplessness and self-pity. I had seen enough. I had experienced enough. I was not going to sit and cry and add to the stress of Grandpa and Mum. I was going to face life head on. I was going to break that cycle and come out of it. I had every reason to do it if not for anyone but for Joy. He was my baby brother and looked up to me. I had to do it for him and for myself.

I told everyone that I was going back to Bhubaneswar. That relieved everyone. I packed my bags and left the next day.

I carried the strength of Grandpa's words with me. Things didn't change much but I changed myself. I was a little stronger mentally, a little more determined, and more focused on not letting rotten thoughts touch me.

I made sure I had my blinders on.

One evening, I had an argument with one of the girls who had never liked me and she said I came from a broken family. I blew a flying kiss at her and left the room.

I wasn't bothered by the word "broken family" anymore. What did it really mean anyways? Not having one parent can't mean a broken family. I certainly had a full family, a great mother, amazing grandparents, cousins, uncles, and aunts. I understood it well now and I was glad. I felt stronger and kinder in a strange way, both at the same time.

I started a routine of going out for evening walks all by myself. It gave me a confidence that I had never experienced before. I wrote every single day. My thoughts. My goals. About life. I fell in love with Calculus during my undergraduate days. I found Multivariable Calculus and Linear Algebra fascinating. Vector functions and Partial Derivatives made me strong. In a way I liked that. The more I learned, the hungrier I became. I spent all my free time writing and solving problems. I wrote letters to Grandpa every week and he wrote me back. There started a new chapter in my life.

Debating Club

With that new chapter in my life, I was more positive and marched ahead with more vigor. In the next six months, I managed to make a few good friends. I liked one girl in particular, Sonnie. We loved going to the beach during our free time and eating fish fry. Isn't that the truth of life? We don't need many friends, just one good friend. One friend to stand by your side when you feel low.

During the sophomore year of my undergraduate days, I came up with the idea of "Debating Club," similar to what my father had started during his college days in Delhi.

It was a club where any girl was welcome to join anytime. We picked a topic and discussed it the following Friday. Most of the subjects we picked were related to the political systems, fall of dynasties, democracy, and world history. The number of members in the club grew from two to twenty in just one month.

I wrote a long letter detailing my "little triumphs" to Grandpa. He sent me a letter back saying what I did was the right thing. Grandpa's letter made me confident about accepting others who were not like me.

People say "human beings" are complicated creatures, but for me, at that point of time, human beings were the simplest creatures.

Life was good as there were few complications and more time to focus on what I wanted to do with my life. I still maintained my old diary and wrote every day. Sometimes, I went to the public library near my hostel. Studying in the library was my ultimate paradise.

I had started to like my imperfect life; all the miracles and the blessings, as well as the not so nice things

It was the Spring of 1999, winter was almost over. Days were getting warmer and longer. We used ceiling fans in our rooms, and they made noises. Few girls in the club found the noise annoying, so Sonnie suggested if we could do the meeting on the terrace that Friday evening.

We had not picked up any particular topic that evening, but instead we were going to recite some of the most inspiring speeches. Winston Churchill's "We Shall Fight on The Beaches," Mahatma Gandhi's "Quit India," Nelson Mandela's speech in 1990 after he was released from the prison. I picked Abraham Lincoln's "Gettysburg Address." To me, it was surreal! How deeply was I moved by that speech! I had read those lines many times before but had never recited it in front of people. By the end of that semester, I had read more than ten biographies on President Lincoln.

Later that night, we collected money and bought pastries for everyone.

"What will happen to this debating club after we leave, Lisa?" Sonnie asked.

"I don't know," I said and paused for some time.

"I hope someone picks up the thread and continues it," I said.

Internet was a new technology those days, and there were only a handful of internet booths in Bhubaneswar. All of them had dial-in internet, and it took forever for the connection to be established.

One evening, Sonnie and I went to a nearby booth to open our first email I.Ds. We waited for a long time and once the dial-in internet was connected, we opened our first Yahoo IDs.

"Wow! We will be able to stay in touch with each other even after college," I said.

"Yes, for sure. But I sincerely hope that many years down the line, they will have something sophisticated, not these dial-in connections."

We laughed and walked on the beach for the whole evening.

When I came back to the dorm, Mum was waiting for me.

"Maa, I am so happy to see you here."

"Me, too, Lismun. I have come to take you home for few days."

"Home? Is everything okay, Maa?"

"Not really."

We went back to Sambalpur the next day. Grandpa was down with Malaria and he could hardly remember anything.

1998–1999

I stayed in Sambalpur for a few days and my presence gave Mum a lot of strength. Shanti came for dinner one evening and when she greeted Grandpa with a warm hello, he couldn't recognize her.

"You remember Shanti, Grandpa?" I asked him.

"Who is Shanti?"

I looked at Mum helplessly and we both knew that he was slipping into dementia.

When I was in high school, Grandpa was in the pink of health. He was just a happy man. He never had any major health problem. Every now and then, he talked about some mild pain in his joints. But that was about it.

I reminded Grandpa of all the times we had spent together but he just couldn't recollect anything. He knew all my friends, not just Shanti, but now, he couldn't even remotely recollect anyone's name.

A few days later, I went for an evening walk with Grandpa. Grandma had asked us to buy some eggplants while coming back.

When we were at the market, I asked Grandpa, "Let's get some white and purple eggplants."

"I think we need to buy spinach leaves," he said.

I looked at him and he looked confused and tired.

When we ate dinner that night, Mum was crying.

"You okay, Maa?"

"Yes, I am fine. It was nice that you stayed with me for a few days. I was a little stressed out. This is too much for me. It pains to see Grandpa so helpless."

"I can understand, Maa. I can stay for a few more days if you want."

"No, you go back. You need to go back and finish your course, Lisa. I am here. I will take care of Grandpa," Mum said.

"Yes, Maa."

I went back to Bhubaneswar to finish my semester and Mum got busy taking care of Grandpa.

It was around that time, I met Ajjai. He was a fourth-year medical student and called himself "A.J." We spent a lot of time talking to each other. He was intelligent and caring. He was studying in a different city and we could not meet often, so we wrote to each other regularly.

Grandpa's Painful Struggle with Alzheimer's

By 1999, Grandpa had lost a lot of his memory. He couldn't write words, speak complete sentences or talk clearly.

I was scheduled to leave for Bombay in June 1999 for my summer training at Philips India Ltd. My train was in the evening and I spent the whole morning sitting by Grandpa's side. He was busy writing something on the notebook. I couldn't understand a single word he had written.

"What are you writing?" I asked him while putting moisturizer on his dry toes.

"A letter to my granddaughter."

"How nice! Where is she?"

"She studies in a different town."

"Do you miss her?"

"Yes. I do. We all do."

"All? Who else?"

"Other people who live in this house."

"Who are those people?"

"I don't know their names."

I laughed and cried at the same time.

Mum accompanied me to Bombay. When we were in the overnight train, I wrote a few letters to Grandpa. Mum spent a week with me in Bombay and returned back to Sambalpur. I gave her the letters and told her to read them to Grandpa, one letter a day.

I spent six weeks in Bombay working as an intern. It was an enriching experience and I made a little money. I took great pride in buying a blue shirt for Grandpa with my first hard earned money.

When I came back to Sambalpur after my training, it was a Monday afternoon and Mum and Joy were both in their respective schools. Grandpa and Grandma were eating lunch. Grandpa looked at me and said, "Welcome home, Lisa."

I was touched by his gesture and was pleasantly surprised that he remembered my name. I joined them for lunch. Grandpa's fine motor skills had deteriorated a bit. He spilled food around his plate when he ate.

"Can I feed you with this spoon?" I asked him.

"Yes," he said while looking at his plate.

I fed him lunch that day. I was content.

Grandpa had started a weird habit around that time; he moved the furniture around the house during the night. One of the things he did was to move the sofa and side tables from one place to another place. But even then, he was very careful. He never broke anything or destroyed any artifact.

Mum and Grandma found it frustrating. One morning, Grandma said, "I am tired of this."

"It will be all okay, Grandma," I told her.

"No, it will never be okay. Your Grandpa is never going to be the same."

We both knew that what she said was right.

Grandpa woke up many times in the night and everyone in the house was sleep deprived.

That's when Mum made a difficult decision. She decided to take a break from work. She stayed home to take care of Grandpa fulltime.

One week later, I went back to Bhubaneswar. During the final year of engineering, a lot of my classmates were getting ready for the placement tests to work in Bangalore and Hyderabad in the information technology field. I hadn't made any concrete plan yet and was in two minds. Some of my classmates were planning on writing the graduate record examinations to go to the United States for higher studies. Time was the key and the clock was ticking. I felt that I was caught between two minds and I needed some coffee.

I spoke to A.J. about it and he said, "I am applying for my passport. I would like to apply for residency somewhere in the US."

After a couple of months and looking at some other options, I made my decision. I was going to the United States of America for higher studies. That evening, I went to the book store to get a G.R.E. book to study for the test.

When A.J. came to meet me in January 2000, we went to the beach and spent an entire day talking. When we were coming back, he proposed, and I said yes. It was the happiest day of my life.

I finished Engineering in 2000 and I found a job in Bhubaneswar within a couple of months. I stayed as a paying guest at a distant relative's house. The place was fully furnished, and I didn't have to buy any furniture. The best part was that I shared the meals with them, too, and didn't have to cook. I loved it because I did not like cooking.

All I had to do was to give them a check at the end of month. A few months later, I filled up my G.R.E. exam registration fees.

I needed some Kaplan C.Ds. When I told Uncle Himansu and Aunt Renu about it, they assured me that they would take care of it. My uncle's friend,

Paul, was a professor in Montreal, Canada. He ordered it for me within twenty hours. The total cost was around $80. Once I had installed the software and I had my Kaplan C.Ds ready, I got busy with the practice tests. I had made a routine for myself and I tried sticking to the schedule as much as I could.

2001

A.J. left for the U.S. in June 2001. I decided to apply for schools next year fall.

Meanwhile, Joy got through the Indian Institute of Technology entrance examination and joined the best engineering college in India, IIT Kharagpur for his undergraduate studies.

Things in Sambalpur had changed a lot around 2001. Grandpa had developed Alzheimer's in full swing. Grandma was overwhelmed with the responsibilities and she kept to herself mostly. Uncle Bhanja often came and stayed with my grandparents during that time. Taking care of everyone in the house made Mum exhausted and I knew it well. But she was trying her best. I called her from Bhubaneswar every day.

"How are you, Mum?" I asked her during one of my routine calls.

"I am good," Mum cried on the phone and hung up on me.

I couldn't sleep that night. I wanted to be there for Mum, so next day, I went back to Sambalpur.

"Lisa, you can't study for your exam here," Mum said.

"I want to be with you, Maa."

"There will be distraction here."

"I will be okay."

Mum was happy initially when I came back. But things changed and she started to snap over small things. She would get mad for no reason.

Sometimes, it was, "Why did you put the wet towel there?" Sometimes, it was, "I am so tired and taking care of everyone. You need to help me as much as possible."

And I did. But I think deep inside Mum knew that she had become irritable. She felt alone and isolated. I often wondered if fear and courage didn't stem from the same source. Maybe they didn't. Maybe they did, maybe her anger and irritations were the suppressed feelings deep inside her heart.

But amidst all the chaos, the most painful part was to see Grandpa helpless. He didn't remember my name. He didn't recognize the name "Lisa." And that hurt me the most.

One evening, as I sat down to do my practice tests, Grandpa came and knocked at the door.

"Come in, please," I said.

"I want to sit by your side."

"Yes, please do, Grandpa."

"Yeah."

"Do you want to learn something?"

"Yes."

"What would you like to do?"

"I don't know," he said while looking at the computer desktop screen closely.

"Well, how about drawing pictures?"

We spent an hour drawing pictures on the computer. He had happy tears in his eyes when I tucked him into bed that night.

We never locked our room doors. One day, I found Grandpa sitting on the sofa and crying. I held him tight.

"Why are you crying, Grandpa?"

"I don't know," he said.

As his granddaughter, it was hard for me to see him go through that. I had never realized the importance of time until then. Those few months with Grandpa changed everything I thought about life and things around me.

Time, just like ocean waves, has its highs and lows. But once it crashes on the shore, it is gone. That's why I wanted to hold on to time and I spent my free time with Grandpa. He refused to go out for walks, so I took him to the terrace every evening.

My life was uncertain. I had resigned my job and was apprehensive about my G.R.E. score and getting admitted to some of the American Universities I was applying to.

A.J. called me every week and sent me a list of the Universities I could apply. I had a dial-up internet at home those and had good connectivity after ten in the night. I sat down every night and spent some time looking at the universities and their engineering departments. But there were nights when I felt anxious.

At home, I had nobody to talk to as Mum's plate was full, and she was busy. Sometimes, I talked to Grandpa, even though I knew he didn't understand a thing I said. He stared at me with his mouth open and smiled occasionally. It was odd in the beginning as he had never been like that when I was growing up, but then I got used to it.

Talking to Grandpa and holding his cold hands inspired me to study harder. I guess that's the good thing about people you love; they continue to bring out the best in you even when they do it unknowingly.

Just a month before my exam, Grandpa started becoming anxious, and he liked it when I was by his side. When I locked the door to practice the Kaplan series tests, he hated it and knocked at the door continuously. I have to admit there were times when I questioned my decision to come to Sambalpur.

"I am not sure if I have made the right choice of coming here," I told Mum crying one night.

"You knew about this situation, Lismun."

"I know. But I need good scores to get admissions from colleges."

"My hands are full, Lisa. I don't know how to help you," Mum said candidly.

I couldn't see any other way, so I decided to hang in there. In spite of my frustrations and all the problems at home, in my hearts of heart, I considered it a privilege to be with Grandpa at that point of life.

I spent most evenings with him for a couple of hours while Mum cooked dinner. After dinner, I kept my nose to the grindstone. I was determined to do well on my test. It was my life and I was going to enjoy the blessings and challenges with equal zest, I told myself every day.

Grandpa was a tea drinker. By that time, I had become an expert in making French fries, too.

"I like that," Grandpa said.

"You mean potato fries?" I said smilingly.

"Yes," he said with a toothless grin.

Every evening it became our daily ritual to have tea and fries. Once in a while, guests came to meet Grandpa. I took great pride in making snacks for them because it filled my heart to see that Grandpa was still loved.

When people talked about old days, it brought a smile on his wrinkled face. I knew he liked being surrounded by people.

But there were times when Grandpa didn't enjoy being with people. It was like he felt alone and sad. One evening he was surrounded by some people and he looked uncomfortable.

"Can we go from here?" he whispered in my ear.

"Yes, Grandpa."

When he wanted to be alone, I sat with him and he liked holding my hand while he fell asleep. I played all sorts of games with him, where he had to reply and tell me answers. Sometimes, he talked but sometimes, he was quiet.

His words were clear and sounded good, but some of his sentences did not make sense. At times, I felt that he had the same expression on his face no matter what I told him.

Grandpa had always enjoyed reading newspapers and writing short stories. Once he lost his memories, it was painful to watch him stare at papers blankly. I read books to him loudly. But soon I realized, he did not understand anything.

Sometimes, I felt that he struggled to find out what I was saying by watching my lip movements. But at times, he was tired of trying. It was the most heartbreaking thing I had ever witnessed.

He loved it when I stroked his back. I told him stories like we tell small kids. I made sure all my stories had happy endings. Grandpa always had a smile at the end. Sometimes, I felt he wanted to express something but couldn't, so I just nodded my head.

One evening, around fourteen of Grandpa's relatives stopped by to see him. Mum was the perfect hostess and cooked dinner for everyone. There was a huge pile of dirty dishes on the kitchen sink. I offered to clean it all. Mum was tired and she went to sleep. I swept the kitchen floor, cleaned the counters, arranged the cloth towels, wiped the stove with soap, and water. It took me a long time and by the time I was done, it was past midnight.

Just before going to sleep, I peeked into my grandparents' room to make sure they had their blankets on.

No, they weren't sleeping soundly. Far from it. They were both awake, drenched in sweat. They were sitting at the edge of the bed, counting the stars. What I saw at that moment was impossible to describe.

My grandparents, who had raised me, were sitting on their bed at the middle of the night and were looking at the sky from their bedroom window.

I went inside, switched on the lights, and kissed their heads. And sat down between them. Grandma smiled and said, "We are looking at the sky."

"And counting the stars?" I added.

"Yes," Grandpa was excited.

"He keeps forgetting how to count after 5," Grandma said.

"It's okay. I will help him."

We were vulnerable and a little insane. But it was so much fun. The vulnerability and insanity were totally worth it. I do not remember how long we sat there, but I remember being myself, happy and content.

Soon it was the wee hours of the morning. When the sun finally rose from the east, Grandpa said, "I miss my granddaughter when I see the sun."

I felt a lump in my throat.

"I think we should all go to sleep now," I cried while tucking them in, "Let's get some rest."

"My granddaughter is like you, she cries for small things," he said while wiping my tears.

"Go to sleep now. Your granddaughter is lucky to have an amazing Grandpa like you," I said while wiping his.

Grandpa's Deteriorating Health

My free time was solely for my grandpa and I loved it that way. Alzheimer's had taken a toll on him, not just his mind but also on his soul. Some days, he looked so sad that it was impossible to imagine that he was the same person who taught me everything about life. He just blankly stared at the ceiling.

But during evenings, he liked sitting on his rocking chair in the terrace. He liked the warmth in the air and quietness of the third floor. When I told him, it was time to go, he didn't budge so we sat down for some more time and it happened every single day.

He needed help while climbing the stairs and getting down. I held his wrinkly and soft hands. He made a face, clearly showing that he didn't like being dependent on anyone. I knew that was painful for him. It was painful for me, too. His helplessness broke my heart a little more.

It was a roller coaster ride for all of us. I think it hit Mum the hardest because to be convinced that her father, who was her greatest inspiration, was not the same person anymore.

Yet, Mum interacted with him as if he understood things. That was a sight to be treasured. It took immense courage and patience to answer his childlike questions and Mum had abundance of it. Her love and dedication towards her parents were unconditional.

But Mum knew she needed an outlet. So, every evening, she would grab her bag to make a quick trip to the local market. One evening, I accompanied her. Like old days, I offered to carry the bags for her. She was more than happy. While coming back, I asked her, "How do you manage to be so patient with Grandpa?"

"It is simple, Lisa. I don't know about other people, but with Grandpa, the real person is still with him. It's just that we can't see him."

Mum and I went to Hyderabad in February 2002. Once I was done with my G.R.E., I waited for two seconds to see my score on the computer screen. I had a great score and I knew I would be getting admission from any college I apply to. I breathed a sigh of relief and walked out of the testing center with a huge smile on my face.

When I was back in Sambalpur, I was sleep deprived. I took a break for two days. I did nothing. I ate, slept, and watched television. I knew I was going to be alright. The important battle was done and over.

Once my energy and vigor were back, I sat down with Uncle Himansu and jotted down a plan and timeline of the things I was going to do. He helped me write the essay for the school applications. I applied for a loan of $5000 and he was my co-signer. I was eternally grateful to him for the help he provided me when I needed it the most in my life.

Deep within me, my mind was entangled in a battle that I didn't know what the answer was. As a human being, I had grown used to my hometown, Sambalpur. My decision to leave India, not just Sambalpur, was a difficult one. I had gotten used to a life; the food, the culture, the mundane day to day things. And now I had made this plan of leaving everything to move to a different country.

The more I thought about it, the sadder I became. March was still pleasant in my hometown. It wasn't very hot. I loved the evening breeze. The air carried the fragrance of raw mangoes. How much I loved it! Grandpa enjoyed being outside the house. I convinced him to go for short walks. Those were the sweetest days.

July 2002, Kolkata, India

I applied to six universities and got my admission letters from all of them. They were called I-20s. My papers were in place, my loan for $5000 was approved, and I was all set. Finally, I decided to go to University of Maryland, College Park because that's where A.J. was.

My visa Interview was on the 2nd of July, 2002. I had all my papers neatly stacked in a file. There were seven people ahead of me. My interview lasted for around fifteen minutes. At the end of the interview, I was told that my student visa had been approved and they would send it to my home address in Sambalpur.

When I was in Kolkata, I stopped by at a nearby store to buy Grandpa a green, striped t-shirt. I checked my wallet, I had just enough money to purchase it.

When we came home, I wrapped a gift paper around it and gave it to Grandpa. He loved it so much that he wore it for three straight days. He refused to take it off. Seeing him so happy made me happy, too.

Within a week, I got my passport back with my visa neatly stamped on it. I bought a navy-blue suitcase. My uncle gave me one of his old suitcases that he had used while doing his Ph.D. in England some eighteen years back. It saved me some money and served its purpose. That's it. That was the luggage I carried when I came to the US; two suitcases!

The night before I left Sambalpur, I was also saddened by the fact that I was going so far away from my grandparents. I sat with them for a long time. All three of us held each other and cried. As I held their wrinkled hands and looked into their sad eyes, I realized how much I loved them. It was my love for them that tore my heart into a thousand pieces. And there was no way to show. I could see my own face in their eyes. They held my hands tight. Grandma wasn't someone who showed emotions often. But that night it was different.

I fed the last dinner to Grandpa. My biggest fear at that moment was that I would never see them again. So, when my pain of leaving them was accompanied by my fear, I felt drained. I was going on a student visa and I had no idea when I was going to come back.

The uncertainty of my future complicated my already tangled thoughts. But I had to let it go. I loosened my grip a little more, but my grandparents held my hands. It was such a difficult situation and Grandpa didn't let me go until Mum came and coaxed him to go to bed.

The next day, we left Sambalpur. Just before leaving, I touched Grandpa's feet, and he blessed me by touching my head. I didn't believe in touching anyone's feet until then, but Grandpa was the greatest man I had ever met. I didn't have the courage to look into his eyes. As I walked out of the house, I cried and didn't look back. Mum and Joy came with me to Bhubaneswar. It was an overnight bus. I didn't feel like talking to anybody.

Once we reached Bhubaneswar, I stayed at Aunt Renu's place for few days. I had just enough savings to buy myself a one-way flight ticket from Kolkata to Dulles International airport. With the leftover money, I bought some good clothes, a pair of shoes, a nice purse, nothing branded or fancy, just a good one. I was all set.

Mum, Joy, Uncle Himanshu, Aunt Renu, and Litun accompanied us to Kolkata to see me off. Things had changed so much in one year. Life just zoomed by and I didn't have time to breathe. We took an overnight train to Kolkata and I had mixed feelings throughout that night.

Litun and I spoke and didn't sleep a wink that night. We talked and talked. She was and will always be my best cousin.

We spent a day in Kolkata eating and shopping some items. My British Airways flight was early in the morning on the 19th of July, 2002. I was twenty-five and I had never traveled out of the country. My flight was at three o'clock in the morning, like most International flights from India. I had a long thirty-two-hour journey ahead of me. Once I got my boarding pass and seat number, I hugged everyone tight and said bye.

I went straight ahead and then thought about Mum for a second. I turned back one last time. I had seen her standing tall many times but that day it was different. I saw her fighting back tears, yet proud. Mum and her towering personality; unwavering, undefeated, unbeaten, unscathed, and unbowed.

I gave her a flying kiss and walked towards the gate with happy tears in my eyes. At that point, I wanted my identity to be her daughter, only her daughter.

My First Flight

Once I stepped inside the plane and found my seat, I felt a rush of pride inside me. I had never traveled in a plane before, not even a domestic flight, and here I was, travelling abroad for higher studies.

As my flight soared up in the open sky, I looked outside and thought about Grandpa and Mum and the countless sacrifices they had made for me to be able to take that flight.

When the air hostess came to offer me a drink sometime later, she found me crying. When she called me for the first time, I didn't hear. So, she ran and got a senior air hostess to talk to me.

"Are you okay, ma'am?" the senior air hostess asked.

"I am not quite sure. I am happy and sad; both at the same time."

"I see. Why don't you tell me why you are sad first?" she said while offering me blanket.

"Because I don't know when will I see my grandpa and Mum next."

"Oh, that's not a problem. You take this same British Airways flight and come back home anytime you wish."

We both laughed and then she made me the best coffee in the world.

There was an elderly gentleman sitting by my side. He looked at me and said, "I have some books. Do you want to read one?"

I looked at him and he smiled.

I asked him, "Are you going to Washington D.C., too?"

He said, "No. Are you?"

"Yes."

"I am British. I am going to London. That's where you change your flight, right?"

I said, "Yes."

I tried sleeping. When I closed my eyes, all I could see was my grandpa's face and his hand reaching out for me and I became restless. I opened my eyes and looked out again. Somewhere amidst the clouds, I saw Mum waving at me. The feeling of pride was back. I could talk to the clouds and fly with them.

I promised myself that making my own self happy was going to be my priority because that was the only way I was going to make Grandpa happy.

I exchanged few more words with the clouds and the sun shone brightly. It was dawn. I was beginning to transform to be person I had always dreamt to be; bright and independent.

If someone came and asked me at that point if there was anything I wanted to change in my life, my answer would have been, "None!"

U.S.A.

I reached in the U.S. on the 19th of July night because I was traveling west. I was on a student visa to the University of Maryland, College Park. I had nothing but my clothes in two suitcases and my university admission letter.

I arrived at the Dulles International Airport in Virginia after a long halt at Heathrow Airport in London. A.J. was there to pick me up. Seeing his bright face gave me the assurance that I was going to be alright.

I called Mum and told her I was safe and sound. We got married two days later on the 21st of July in the presence of some of our friends.

At twenty-five, there began the first chapter of my new life in a foreign country; a graduate student of telecommunications at the University of Maryland. A.J. and I rented a small one-bedroom apartment near the campus.

Broke but Happy

At the end of the day, we were poor graduate students. We put a thick comforter on the wooden floor and it became our bed. For us, it really didn't matter that we didn't have a bed. We had each other and that's what it took to create our beautiful world.

A.J. was writing U.S. M.L.E. exams, mandatory exams for physicians to join residency. We spent many nights studying in the library. Some nights, we were done studying by midnight. The last school shuttle left the campus around eleven in the night. So, when we were done late in the night, we rented a cab. Those were priceless days.

We had a few friends but mostly we kept to ourselves. Nobody told us how to steer our ship and we were our own captains. We had each other to pep ourselves and look up to.

The best thing was that we always looked for interesting projects to do together. A.J. was a good dancer and he taught me some amazing dance moves. I taught him some old Bollywood songs.

We had a fixed budget for food, for renting movies, eating out, house bills, and clothes. I think the thing that hit me real hard was that I didn't have enough money to buy phone cards to call Mum.

"I want to set aside $50.00 every month to call Mum," I told him.

"Yes, that's fine," he assured me lovingly.

"Don't forget to keep $30 every month aside for pumpkin pie," I said and he nodded with a smile.

What I loved about the US was that nobody cared to know about my family. One of my classmates, Rachel, once asked me, "So, Lisa, what do you like most about this country?"

"Do you really want to know the answer?" I asked her.

"Yes," she said.

"Well, what I like here is that nobody asks about my father. In India, when I met people, the first question I was asked was, 'What does your father do?'"

"Wow!"

I smiled. And it was true. I took great pride in telling people about me and what I did.

But there were times I missed home. I would be walking and start crying out of nowhere. I wanted to go Sambalpur and meet everyone back home, but unfortunately, I never had more than $100 in my bank account. The average price of a two-way ticket to India was around $1300.00 and I could never save that much money. So, the easier way to cope with my homesickness was to write letters to Mum.

No matter how busy I was, I took one hour off every Sunday to write letters to Mum. She had a desktop in Sambalpur but no internet and I knew Mum waited for my letters. My letters meant the world to her.

I fell in love with that small college town almost immediately. It didn't take more than twenty minutes to go from one end to another. I didn't have the money to buy a car, but it wasn't a problem as the public transport was good. Every once in a while, I liked taking the subway to downtown D.C.

I was never a big fan of scarves, but during my first fall in Maryland, I bought a couple of woolen ones. A perk of studying in graduate school was meeting people from various countries with different backgrounds. That was the first time I realized how small I was, how insignificant my problems were. As I made more friends, I understood that I wasn't the only one missing home. There were many like me.

I found a graduate assistantship in the Department of Linguistics within three weeks. I started work two days after I was interviewed. That was a huge relief for me. It also meant that I wasn't going to have to pay for tuition for my master program, except for the mandatory fees at the beginning of the fall and spring semesters. On top of that, I got a stipend and a biweekly check for $450 after taxes.

My university scholarship paid up to twelve credits, so I wanted to make the most of that opportunity. That's why I took a number of M.B.A. courses along with M.S. courses. As I was also working twenty hours a week, it got hectic at times. And I loved it.

Initial Days, Fall 2002

At home, I liked that A.J. was focused, sincere, funny, and serious about his future. He inspired me. But more than anything else, being in love was a wonderful feeling. We were inseparable for the next few months. We ate lunch together and waited for each other at the bus stop. He bought me a beautiful, long, black coat before winter. He was protective about me and held my hand while crossing the road. I loved those small gestures.

My initial days outside of home were also amazing. I loved the beautiful fall colors in Maryland. The orange, yellow, red, and green leaves had the heavenly look. It was a treat for the eyes! Walking in the mall in front of the McKeldin Library at the University of Maryland was something that I found interesting. There was a fountain in front of the library. Sometimes, I stopped by to see my own refection in its water. The fall semester was about to start and the whole campus was buzzing with students. I saw parents, too, who had come to drop their kids for the freshman year in the dorms.

I loved the Clarice Smith Performing Art center. I attended some of their plays and dance programs. It was a completely new concept for me because most of the colleges and schools in India didn't have a performing art center.

When I was growing up, I had only two career choices; either engineering or medicine. It was a welcome change for me to see that there were bright students who studied theater, music, and dance to build their careers in those fields.

The first time I walked to the main administration building to register my name and pay the mandatory fees, I cried all the way. There were a few trays of chocolate chip cookies and glazed donuts on the front table to welcome new students. I picked one from each tray. The lady at the counter looked at me and asked, "International student?"

I said, "Yes."

"From India?"

"Yeah."

"You can take two from each tray. I know you kids have come so far from home to study."

I hugged her tight. She kissed my forehead and said, "You will be all right. This experience will make you stronger. Do well and make your parents proud."

"I will," I said as I walked out of the door with all the sweet treats in my hand. I had put mascara on my eyes and it was totally smeared around my face. As I walked towards the bus stop, a couple of people asked if I was doing okay. That's when I realized I needed to go to the restroom to wash my face.

There was a student from Taiwan, Chen. It didn't take long for her to become my best friend. Her family back home was wealthy and she was one of the very few students in our batch to buy a car. Chen and I had lot of things in common. We both loved shoes without heels, good food, and we were voracious readers. But we were also very different from each other. She was an early morning person and I was a night owl. She loved to cook and I didn't enjoy cooking at all.

She found me crying near the door step one morning and asked, "What's wrong?"

"Nothing. Just missing Mum," I said with a faint smile on my face.

"You can call me Mum, if that helps," she said.

We laughed so hard after that.

If Chen was not studying, then she was cooking. Every once in a while, she invited me to dine with her. She cooked delicious vegetable noodles in chicken broth.

Grandpa's Death

Grandpa's health started to decline after I left India. I asked about him every week when I called Mum. Sometimes, Mum called him on the phone, so I could hear his voice. He liked holding the phone without saying anything.

"Say something, father," Mum coaxed him.

"Aaaaa," he said slowly.

I was happy that I could hear his voice. Mum told me that he didn't go to the terrace anymore and preferred being in his room. He didn't remember anything and couldn't say a single word properly. He didn't know where the bathroom and bedroom were and his condition worsened every passing day.

One of those days Mum cried on the phone and said, "I don't know what to do."

"What happened, Maa?" I asked her lovingly.

"There is this filthy smell in the house because Grandpa has pooped in his pants and had walked in the house without cleaning himself."

A few days later when I called Mum, she told me, "Grandpa spilled rice on the sofa today."

This time she wasn't upset and we both had a hearty laugh.

While Grandpa's health kept deteriorating, Grandma started to become weaker, too. Her health had become fragile and she was mostly lost in her thoughts. She didn't talk to anyone much. It was clear that since she was not able to take care of herself, she was in no condition to care for her husband.

The last straw was in July 2003 when Mum came back from the local market after buying groceries and found Grandpa missing. She went running out of the house, but he was nowhere to be seen in the vicinity. Mum told me that it was the first time she thought she was getting panic attacks.

Someone in the neighborhood told Mum that he saw Grandpa taking a bus to Balangir. Fortunately, there were buses going to Balangir every thirty minutes. Mum took the next bus to go there. After three hours, she found him in the Balangir bus stop, wandering around.

She took an evening bus to bring Grandpa back to Sambalpur. He chose to sit in the last seat of the bus towards the corner, with his hands folded against his chest. He looked tired and sleep deprived. Mum went close to him and patted his back.

"Father, it is time to go home. You need a good night's sleep," Mum said.

That evening, Mum made his favorite dinner, white rice and fish curry. Grandpa went straight to sleep after eating. Next day was Friday. I had worked the whole day building a website for one of the professors in Marie Mount Hall at the University of Maryland, College Park. I had a throbbing headache after spending nearly eight hours non-stop looking at the computer screen. When I got home, it was half past four in the evening. I had an urge to call Mum, even though I knew that it was around two in the morning in India.

"Hello, Maa. Can you please call Grandpa? I want to talk to him now."

"Lismun, it is two in the morning. He is sleeping now."

"Maa, I don't think he is sleeping. Can you please check?"

As I waited on the phone line, Mum went to my grandparents' room, and yes, he wasn't sleeping. He was sitting on a chair, looking at the ceiling. Mum got him on the phone. When she put the phone receiver near his ear, he didn't do his usual blabbering that time.

He said, "Hello, Lisa.".

It was loud and clear. I couldn't believe it. It was the biggest pleasant surprise of my life. I was ecstatic. I had so much to say to him, but I had only a few minutes left in my phone card. "I love you, Grandpa. You are my hero," I said

"Lisa," he said again.

"I love you, Grandpa. I love you so much," I said in tears.

He didn't say anything and just held the phone.

"I love you so much, Grandpa. I will call you tomorrow," I said before ending the call.

Next day morning, I was awakened by a phone call from Mum.

"Hello, Lisa," Mum said.

"Hello, Maa, you put the phone down. I will call you back," I told Mum knowing that international calls, especially to the U.S., were expensive for her.

"Call me now. It is urgent," Mum said before hanging up.

I called Mum immediately.

"Grandpa died two hours ago," she said.

I was so choked that I couldn't utter a single word. Mum and I cried on the phone, but Mum mustered all her courage to tell me what she felt, "Lismun, you are the luckiest grandchild in the world. You will always have his blessings. He loved you the most. Your name was the only name he remembered when he died."

That made me even more sad.

"Bye, Maa," was all I could say.

I wanted my mind to shut down. I felt nothing, as if I were air without any weight. As I journeyed through the day, it took monumental effort to just wipe away my never-ending flow of tears. I pushed myself to get up and go to work.

I don't know how I survived the whole day, but by the evening, I was a mess. A.J. was out for a conference. When he came back to College Park that evening, I was still at work. When I saw him outside my work building, I held him tight and cried out loud.

"Are you okay?" he asked me.

"Grandpa died," I said while howling and crying.

He held me tighter. We sat on a nearby bench and he let me cry. When I calmed down a bit, he said, "Let's go home."

As we walked home from the campus, he held my hands tight. Everything looked blurry. I felt a big vacuum inside my heart. Even though I knew that Grandpa was not doing well when I left India in 2002, I consoled myself that he was alive. But now he was gone. Gone forever! I would never be able to see him again.

My entire world had collapsed with that phone call. I felt it had broken into pieces. I knew no matter how hard I tried, his absence would be a huge void in my life.

I was beyond miserable. Nothing consoled me. Nothing. Grandpa was my inspiration, my idol, my guide, my friend, and my conscience. He meant so much to me. And now he was gone.

The next day, I stayed home. I did nothing. I didn't eat, didn't call anyone. A.J. was working on a paper and he had to go to work. He kissed me goodbye and left.

I stayed in the bed the whole day without food or water. When it was evening and the sun had turned orange during twilight, A.J. came home with some Chinese food. As we sat down to eat, I told him, "I want to go to India."

He said, "Yes, go. I will book the ticket."

I logged into my bank account. The total we had was $180 in both our accounts. I looked at him and said, "I don't know what to do."

"Let's buy the ticket with the credit card."

"But a round-way ticket will cost around $1800."

"That's fine. We will pay off the credit card in a few months."

That was a lot of money and I decided not to go.

Now when I look back, I feel that was a poor decision on my part. But at that moment, I couldn't think of any other solution.

For the first couple of months, I cried a lot, sometimes in the middle of night. Nothing could console me. I loved to see the sun rise during dawn though. It was as if I saw Grandpa's face in the sun.

A few weeks later when my school reopened before Labor Day weekend, I was up the whole night. When it was time to go for my classes, I decided to open the windows and see the birds fly up in the sky, the sun rising among the red clouds, and the dew drops on the leaves. I made a conscious decision to get out of my sadness. I had to do it because I was going insane. I was plain determined to enjoy the ups and downs of life.

I put a picture of Grandpa on my bedside table. I talked to him every day and I heard his replies, or at least, I believed I did.

Beautiful memories are like priceless beads in our favorite necklace. They shine brightly to make us smile. Those sweet memories become our greatest strength during our darkest days and build compassion in our hearts. They fill our hearts with limitless love and plant the seed of gratitude. I was glad that I had the privilege to make those wonderful memories with Grandpa. That was perpetual in my life. Everything else was transient.

Career

When A.J. began the residency program in Baltimore in 2004, we didn't see each other much. We still lived in College Park as I had one more semester to go. A.J. needed a sturdy car to go to the hospital. We had an old car that a dear friend had given us free. It was worth less than $500. Though the car came free, it wasn't free of problems. The car would often break down and the wipers didn't work. Car repair was becoming a big problem.

I looked up the nearest car dealership number and called one of them.

"Hello, my name is Lisa Bedbak. I would like to know the price of a new Toyota Corolla," I said.

"Sure. Let me transfer your call. Hold on," the receptionist said while making a selection for the car salesman.

"Hello, ma'am. What can I do for you?" the car salesman asked.

"We are looking to buy a car, preferably a Toyota Corolla. What's the price range?"

"Yes, we have many Toyota Corollas. Tell me new or pre-owned."

"New."

"Okay. What color are you specifically looking for?"

"I don't know. I am not picky about the color."

"How much down payment?"

"I am sorry. We have no money. Maybe $100."

"And you want to buy a new car?"

"Yes, certainly."

"Okay. No, problem. We can check your credit history. Do you have a credit card? Please give me your S.S.N."

"I am sorry. I have neither a credit card nor a credit history."

The salesman was getting a little restive by now.

"Ma'am, do you have a driver's license?"

"No. Come on, we live in D.C. Public transport is fantastic here. I don't need a driver's license. I never applied for one."

"So, what is this car for?"

"My husband. He is a medical resident and his commute is long, especially on I-95."

The car salesman started to laugh.

"Ma'am, why don't you call me when you have a driver's license and save up some money or even better, please ask your husband to call us."

A.J. was right behind me when the phone conversation was happening. After I switched off my cell phone with a hopeless face, he burst into laughter. I looked embarrassed. He hugged me and said, "Don't worry. I will take care of this one. Okay?"

"Okay," I said.

We waited for two months, saved some money, and bought a white Corolla in Aug, 2004. Our first car. It was quite an achievement.

My Sweet Friend, Amari, 2005

Just before I graduated, we moved to Catonsville, a small suburb in the south of Baltimore. I was writing Cisco certification exams and was busy studying most of the time. It was around that time, I met my neighbor, Claudia. She was in her mid-thirties. She didn't have a car and never came out of the house. She was a single mother and abused her five kids.

Her oldest son was twenty-two years and had moved out of the house. Claudia lived with her three daughters and her youngest son, John, a five-year old little boy. She wasn't very nice to her kids most of the time. To me, they looked like the sweetest kids on earth. Sometimes, I felt like telling her how unfair she was. But then I stopped myself because I didn't have the time to care for the kids and it was none of my business.

Amari was Claudia's third daughter and was a beautiful little girl, around thirteen years old. When I saw her for the first time, I smiled but she never smiled back and kept pretty much to herself.

It was Fall 2005 and I was brisk walking outside my apartment and my husband was still at work. Amari waved *hello* from her apartment window. I smiled back but she went back inside.

Next day, I was at home, just lazing around and watching television. There was a knock at the door. It was her! She was crying.

"Why are you crying, dear?" I asked her.

She wiped her tear and said, "Do you have some butter and eggs at home?"

"I think so. I will check in the fridge. What's your name?"

"Amari."

"Come inside," I let her in. I was making sandwiches. I asked her, "Would you like to have one?"

"Okay," She said, trying to stop sobbing.

"I am Lisa. It's nice to meet you. You can talk to me if you want," I told her in a gentle way as we nibbled our bread and lettuce.

"Nice to meet you, too. But I don't want to talk now," she said looking at the table.

I didn't say anything. To me, Amari was an enigma. There was a glow on her face and she carried beauty and mystery in her eyes. I wanted to talk to her more but I didn't want our friendship to be a forced one.

"I don't have many eggs, just two or three. Will that work?" I said while searching around things in the fridge.

"Yes. I want some butter, too."

"I am sorry I don't have butter."

"That's fine," she said with a sad face.

"Why do you need eggs and butter?" I asked.

"I am going to bake a cake with my sister," she said.

"How nice!"

We talked for some more time. Without a doubt, she had the prettiest smile and big eyelashes.

When she went home that evening, she seemed okay and wasn't crying anymore. I had a feeling that she liked me, at least I hoped that she did, for I fell in love with her. Tremendously.

A few months later, I had a job interview and when I stepped out of the house, it was drizzling. I saw her sitting near the window and watching the rain. She waved at me and I waved back. I didn't understand why she was not in school that day.

A month later when I had to go grocery shopping, I saw Amari playing outside with a tiny red ball in the snow. She wasn't wearing snow pants.

"Do you want to go grocery shopping with me?" I asked her.

"Yes. But I have to ask my mom."

"I will wait for you, Amari. Go and ask."

When she came back a few minutes later, she didn't look happy.

"Are you okay? Are you coming with me?"

"Yes," she said with a grim face.

"Come, hop in."

When she sat in the car, I asked her again, "Are you okay?"

"I am fine. My Mom wants me to come back soon because I have to cook dinner."

We were both quiet after that. I had an audio C.D. playing in the car of a prominent singer from India, Jagjit Singh.

"What language is this?" Amari asked me.

"Hindi. That's the national language in India."

That's what I loved most about Amari, her curiosity. She wanted to know about anything and everything around her.

We bought some Indian groceries. She had never been to a store like that before, so she was filled with inquisitiveness. She wanted to know the names of the spices.

"Cinnamon, Turmeric, and Cardamom," I said.

I told her little bit about Indian culture and the languages. She was surprised to know that most Indians were multi-lingual. The more I spoke, the more her eyes twinkled.

"Do you think you have enough time to go to a bakery store?" I asked her.

"Really?" she was pleasantly surprised.

After we were done, we went to a cake shop. We ordered a few slices of banana bread and some drinks.

"Do you cook dinner every day?" I asked her because I had an unsettling feeling that I couldn't control.

"Most days. Some days Jackie makes it."

"Jackie is?"

"My sister."

"When do you do your homework?"

"I don't know. Never…I guess."

"What?" I asked her. It was unbelievable.

"You should do your homework every day."

"I find math difficult."

"You can come to me and I will teach you."

While going back home, I bought a German chocolate cake for her. We were late by some thirty minutes or so. I was scared for her. When we reached in the apartment complex, I decided to walk with her up to her house. Jackie opened the door and went back to the kitchen without saying a word.

"I am sorry Amari is late. My mistake. I took her to a couple of new places," I told Claudia.

"Okay," she said. From her looks, I could make it up that she wasn't happy.

"I am really sorry. Entirely my mistake."

"I don't like Amari going out in the evenings. She makes dinner for me and I like my dinner to be prepared in a particular way. Amari is good at that."

"She is only thirteen. Why does she have to cook dinner for you? She needs to go to school and do her homework."

"I am sick. I can't get up from here. How the hell am I going to cook?"

"Please do something about it. Find someone to take care of you. Your kids cook, clean, and do everything around the house. Look, Amari's life is priceless, and she has her whole future in front of her. Please let her be a kid and let her thrive."

"Don't lecture me here. Get out of my house," she said with an angry face.

I left their house with a heart wrenching feeling. My sheer inability to help the little girl I loved so dearly made me frustrated that night.

As far as I was concerned, I had finished my masters then and was looking for jobs. I had a few job offers, but they were all outside of Maryland and I wanted to be in Maryland because that's where my husband was working. I had applied for a couple of jobs in the Maryland-Virginia area, and I was waiting for interviews. At the meantime, I was also writing cisco certification exams.

One weekend, Amari surprised me when she told me that for her school essay, she wrote about India.

"My topic was 'India—a culturally vibrant country.' I did all the research on my own. I walked to the library to get the books since I didn't have a laptop."

That genuinely impressed me. My first job was in a multi-national company in downtown DC. Some days I also worked from Northern Virginia. I loved my job. My husband was doing his residency, where he was slogging for eighty to eighty-five hours a week, so I got busy with work, too. The commute didn't bother me much. I didn't have a car. We had only one car that my husband drove. Driving south on I-95 was always too much hassle as it was crowded. I took the subway and preferred it. I could read or take a short nap.

But the downside was that I hardly saw Amari. During the weekends, I did nothing but sleep as I was so sleep deprived. As my husband was working nearly crazy hours in the hospital, we got up late during the weekends. How we loved it! Most Sundays, we got up at lunch time.

One weekend, I realized that I had three loads of laundry to do. I had no clean clothes to wear the next week. So, once I was up and had fed myself, I decided to get going on the laundry thing. The apartment complex had a common Laundro-wash. I had a long wait, so I sat in one corner to send few emails. Thank God I had the V.P.N. connection. Someone came from behind and hugged me. It was Amari.

"Hey, how are you? What's going on?"

"I don't know what to say. My Mom hasn't paid the rent for the last three months. So, the leasing office people might throw us out. I haven't been to school in the last few days."

I knew it wasn't rosy and smooth for her, but I hadn't imagined it was that bad. I was expecting my first pay check in a couple of days.

"Look, I don't have anything much right now as you know this is my first job. I can give you fifty dollars now. When I get my salary in two days, I will help you."

"I don't know what will happen."

I kneeled over, looked at her, and said, "Look, sweetie, I love you. Never ever doubt that. Let me help you with some money now. Later, we will see. But, please, don't miss school, no matter what. Do your homework regularly, every day."

We drove to the A.T.M. machine and I gave her $60.00 that afternoon. I kissed her forehead. We ate ice-cream with tears rolling down our cheeks. We had totally forgotten about the laundry thing until someone came and yelled at me to take my load of clothes out of the washer because she had her load to finish.

Amari's sweet face had scars of exhaustion and stress. She never told me, but I could figure it out that she was doing a lot of house work. I saw that somewhere behind the scars, there was a feisty girl who didn't give up. She valued hard work. Her grades had started to improve significantly but now she had stopped going to school. She basically came back to where she had started from. That shattered my spirits.

That week was hectic at work and I hardly had time to think about anything. I wanted to meet Amari that weekend to see how she was doing. I thought of giving her a surprise visit, so I went to her apartment with some money in an envelope. I was shocked to see that her front door was locked and they had left the apartment complex.

It all happened too fast for me to comprehend the severity of it. I felt devastated as I could not see her for the last time.

Even to this day, I often wonder what is she up to and where is she now. I regret not being able to help her much. Gosh, how much I loved her. Not sure why but maybe because she was so much like me.

Next day, when I woke up, I sat on the bed and cried for a couple of hours, like I had a bad dream or something. That's life, I guess. Broken dreams are like thorns; they prick us every now and then and remind us of our inadequacies.

I hope she is doing well wherever she is. I hope God gives her enough strength to fight the battle of life. I hope that she does not become a victim of the vicious cycle of emotional abuse from her own mother. I hope she does not lose her interest in math and music. I hope she finds the true meaning of life wherever she is. I hope she is *happy*!

A month later when I called home, Mum told me that Grandma had a stroke and she was hospitalized. Grandma died seven days later. It was one of the saddest days for me.

My childhood friend, Shanti, was in Sambalpur those days and she gave a lot of support to Mum. I will be eternally grateful to her for that support. Grandma's funeral and last rites were done in Puri, a coastal town in eastern India.

I called Mum two times a day for the next few months, no matter how busy I was. Sometimes I called her while cooking, sometimes while travelling in the train, and sometimes while mopping. I didn't forget to call her no matter how time pressed I was.

Time flew and I got busier with work and commute. I was working on an important Sarbanes Oxley project in the project management office in Fannie

Mae and I constantly worked on controls. It was relatively a new field and I enjoyed being a big part of it.

As months passed, I commuted between Herndon and Tenley Town offices. There was a shuttle between these two offices every thirty minutes and sometimes, I prepared my presentations while travelling. Fannie Mae had provision for dinner for people working after seven in the evening and it was convenient to eat dinner and go home.

Commuting every day from Northern Virginia and D.C. and finally to Baltimore was becoming too long of a commute for me. That's when A.J. and I decided to move back to College Park. We knew that town well. The good thing that came out of it was that, at least, we ate home cooked food during weekends.

Our Unconquerable Hopes, Our Greatest Joys, and Our Brightest Lights, Our Kids

Arjun Was Born, 2006

In 2006, A.J. was a third-year medical resident and we were expecting our first baby in September. Mum traveled from India to help us out. I hadn't seen her since 2002 and I was excited beyond words to see her.

On September 1st, 2006, I left work early and A.J. picked me up from Tenley Town subway station in downtown D.C. We went to Dulles International Airport to pick Mum up. We spent the next three hours hugging and crying. I was allowed to work from home from September 2nd onwards and it was big blessing. Having Mum by my side gave me a lot of strength. We talked, laughed, and cried.

Mum said, "I like how you manage your home and career. We have come a long way."

How true that was! It was surreal. Mum was still the same and had not changed much except some more white hair. I still worked; sometimes sitting on the couch in the living room and sometimes from my bed inside the bedroom. Mum had always enjoyed cooking and she cooked my favorite dishes.

Evenings were pleasant and we went out for short walks. Those were beautiful days.

Arjun was born on the 26th of September, 2006 via C-section. The first time A.J. saw him, he said, "Gosh! He has so much hair."

And then they brought him close to me and I held him tight. It was euphoria. The incredible feelings of joy and pride filled up my heart. My heart was so full and there was no space to have anything else. It was unbelievable. I spent an entire hour studying his ears and face.

Arjun had an aura around him, and it captivated me. He was mine; an extension of my being. And that made me extremely proud.

My little Arjun ruled my life. He could make me cry and he could make me laugh in a split second. He controlled my life. The best part is I loved it. I loved every bit of it. When we brought him home from the hospital, Mum made some coffee for us.

As we sat on the couch and I looked at his cute face again, something inside me changed. It was like I became someone else without even realizing it.

My outlook, my perspective, and my priorities changed. After that day, whenever I made a plan or did something, I put him first. He latched onto every single thought of mine.

The most important change I saw in myself was that I wanted to protect my baby. I wanted to shield him completely from any harm, anything that could remotely hurt him.

When Arjun was one month old, we had a mini celebration at home with cake and candles. After everyone went to sleep, Arjun was up all night because of acid reflux.

During my sleep deprivation and seeing my little boy helpless and throwing up in the night, I wondered about my childhood days. I wondered why my father never felt like what I felt about my son. The sense of belongingness, protection, privilege, and unconditional love I felt for him was out of the world. I had never felt like that about anyone. I wondered why my father wanted to hurt his kids all the time.

Of course, I never got the answers of my questions and deep within, I know I will never get. Those answers will always remain unknown to me, always.

That night as I held Arjun close to me, we both fell asleep while listening to Evgeny Kissin's piano. It was the night I promised that I was going to give my baby all the love in the universe that I never received.

2010

In 2010, we moved to Houston, Texas.

Our second son was born on the 25th of January, 2011 through regular C-section. We named him Anmol, which means priceless in Hindi. He truly is our biggest gift.

The sweetest thing about Anmol was that he smiled all the time. He smiled first thing in the morning when we woke up and he smiled the last thing before going to bed. He had a chubby face and looked straight into my eyes. He was ready to talk to me even before he learnt to speak.

Anmol was the sweetest baby I had ever seen. Needless to say, he became our lifeline the day he was born. When I sat down with Arjun and Anmol together on my lap for the first time, I wondered if they were going to love each other the way Joy and I loved.

With Arjun and Anmol by our side, A.J. and I knew that our little family was complete.

Now we live in Ann Arbor, Michigan. I say, "I love you," to my kids every day and I mean it. It is fun to tickle them, giggle with them, and laugh uncontrollably until our bellies hurt.

Anmol screams the most when I tickle him. We leap, twirl, play, sing, and dance like buffoons sometimes.

It is a blessing to see my kids grow and see them come into their own personalities.

This is my life and everything I had ever dreamt of.

THE END